Praise for
Letters from Dachau

Letters from Dachau *is an important addition to the literature of World War II liberation. Clarice Wilsey gives us a deeply personal account that bravely reveals the human tragedy that was the Holocaust. Through her father's letters, she shares with startling openness the deepest thoughts of a man plunged into one of the world's most horrific crimes. Wilsey reflects on this crucial history as a daughter raised in the shadow of trauma.*

DEE SIMON
BARAL FAMILY EXECUTIVE DIRECTOR,
HOLOCAUST CENTER FOR HUMANITY, SEATTLE

What the courageous doctor could not achieve in a lifetime—speak about the unspeakable—his daughter has done in these pages. In this most original and vivid pulling back of the covers at the wartime bedside, Clarice Wilsey has revealed her father's deep empathy, his capacity to improvise, and his deft skill under fire, all while she explores the tragic cost to his own well-being. Clarice has given her father's service a voice where there was none, a memoir only she could assemble from his rediscovered letters, and a purpose only her hindsight could bestow upon his legacy."

TED BARRIS
AUTHOR,
"RUSH TO DANGER: MEDICS IN THE LINE OF FIRE"

This book is magnificent—powerful, riveting, and remarkably well-researched. The chapters on Dachau are painful to read, of course, particularly because the author chose—wisely, necessarily—to include many of the graphic scenes and accounts her father wrote in his letters to her mom. Wilsey describes people at their best, their worst, their most noble, their most craven. She pulls no punches; war ain't pretty.

Her father is depicted as a brilliant man utterly traumatized by his war-time experiences. Wilsey makes it clear that war doesn't end when the last gun is fired—but, rather, its effects extend to human beings for generations afterward.

It is not beach reading; it is dense with factual material, psychological perplexities, both war time and domestic conflicts, and issues occasioned by her father's unique personality. I am deeply, deeply impressed.

ELIZABETH HULL, PH.D.
POLITICAL SCIENCE PROFESSOR,
RUTGERS UNIVERSITY

This story will break, and then open your heart to a daughter who bravely reveals the contradiction of a father's heroism during World War II and the "unheroism" that he wields at home to his wife and children. Wilsey discloses the truth about her father, a medical doctor, and finds redemption without vengeance in her hope to help other veteran's families.

DIANE CARLSON EVANS
AUTHOR, "HEALING WOUNDS: A COMBAT NURSE'S 10-YEAR FIGHT
TO GIVE WOMEN A PLACE OF HONOR IN WASHINGTON, D.C.

Letters from Dachau
A father's witness of war, a daughter's dream of peace

Clarice Wilsey
with Bob Welch

Duncan
Gardens
Press

Copyright 2020 by Clarice Wilsey

Duncan Gardens Press

All rights reserved. No part of this book may be reproduced in any form without written permission from the author, except by reviewers or authors who may quote brief passages in support of their works.

Front cover: The author, age three, and her father in 1950, backdropped by a photograph Dr. David Wilsey took of Holocaust victims at Dachau concentration camp after his arrival in May 1945.

Back cover: One of the more than 300 letters Wilsey wrote to his wife, Emily.

Back cover photo of the author by Kyle Santos, photographer, Hawai'i.

Front and back cover designs by Bob Welch and Tom Penix.

ISBN: 978-1-7346625-0-4

To contact the author: lettersfromdachau@gmail.com

Printed in the United States of America

To Jason Pillado, with thanks for your service to our country and for your great commitment to veterans, particularly at the University of Oregon. It's been an honor to work with you.

To Professor Gerald Berk, of the University of Oregon, whose father, Dr. Morton Berk, along with my father, Dr. Dave Wilsey, served with distinction after the liberation of the Dachau concentration camp. How incredible to see the photo of our fathers in 1945, right next to each other!

Finally, to my brother and sister, with love.

Foreword

Clarice Wilsey has written an astounding book that not only puts focus on horrific human tragedies during World War II but presents common and debilitating problems regarding the return of war veterans to their families.

Letters from Dachau paints a chilling picture of the atrocities prisoners faced during Hitler's regime during the war. The pictures Wilsey paints with words describe unimaginable sights from the Battle of the Bulge and the liberation of Dachau. Although horror is present in all conflicts, the tragedies discovered at Dachau seem beyond possible in terms of their disregard for human life.

Dr. Wilsey's letters home—some 300 of them—were accurate, descriptive, and captivating—so much so that they qualify as invaluable historical documents. Few men and women in World War II wrote with such insight, candidness, and, at times, humor. Dr. Wilsey's letters were his way of sharing his experience at Dachau—his emotions and his deepest frustrations—with his wife back home. As such, they offer readers a deeper understanding of what war can do to people than most war books that focus heavily on weapons and tactics.

The medical units assigned to the task of helping save the prisoners, which included Clarice's father, were tragically understaffed. Despite that, exhaustion, and rampant disease, they set aside their personal needs and saved as many patients as possible.

At the end of hostilities, it's common for those returning from war—and the person's loved ones—to experience difficulty in finding "normal life" again. Sadly, Captain Wilsey's experience was that and more for his family. The book describes the heartbreak and emotional trauma in a superb way.

In the post-war 1940s, '50s and even '60s, Post-Traumatic Stress Syndrome (PTSD) hadn't even been defined as such. Now, of course, it is a common ailment among war veterans, resulting in, among other things, climbing suicide rates. But, as the author points out, PTSD was not well understood during, or soon after, World War II.

Letters from Dachau is written deeply from the heart. It should be considered as a textbook for college and military studies. And should find its way onto bookshelves and smart screens for the general public to better understand the horrors of Dachau and their lingering effects on those who liberated it—and those liberators' families.

PETER D. HAYES
BRIGADIER GENERAL,
USAF RET.

History, despite its wrenching pain, cannot be unlived, but if faced with courage need not be lived again.
MAYA ANGELOU,
AMERICAN POET, AUTHOR, AND CIVIL RIGHTS ACTIVIST

Prologue

A Note to My Readers

When I first saw the photographs, my heart lurched. It was 1953 and our family of five had just moved into a new house in Spokane, Washington. Amid the chaos of moving, the pictures were in a box that had been temporarily placed on the dining room table.

They were like nothing I'd ever seen before—not that by then I'd seen a whole lot, period. I'd never even had a pet die. I was six. I took a handful of the photos and, sitting on the floor, started going through them, amazed at what I saw. Time stood still in an awkward way. There were pictures of dead people with no clothes on, stacked in piles. Pictures of men in white coats in a long room, bending over people who looked like skeletons. Pictures of—

"Clarice!"

My father's commanding voice shattered the quiet, sending shivers of fear through me.

"Where did you get these?"

I'd never seen him so mad—and I'd often seen him mad, especially at my mother.

"You are *not* to look at these—*ever!* These are not for little girls to see. Do you understand?"

My head nodded, my heart raced. He picked up the box.

"Daddy, who are these people and why don't they—

"Do. You. *Understand?*"

I nodded my head faster. My eyes widened as far as they would go.

He walked away with the box. I shook in fear about something I did not understand—and would not for more than half a century.

* * *

IN THAT SAME house, I grew from a girl to a young woman. I left in 1965 for college at the University of Washington in Seattle. After that the house became just a quick stopover en route to my going somewhere else. I did social work in Kentucky, then followed positions at colleges in Michigan, New York, Iowa, and Oregon. Finally, the house became the place where I returned to visit my aging parents, where I came when my father, David, died in 1996, and where my mother, Emily, died in 2008.

My mother had lived in the house for fifty-six years. In 2009, after her death, my brother and sister and I gathered to prepare the house for sale. We were boxing up what remained of my parents' belongings. At the time, I was sixty-two.

In the back of my mind, I wondered about those photographs I'd seen when I was six; would my parents have kept them? I knew my father had a World War II trunk in the attic. Could the pictures be in it? Or was the trunk even still in the house? As my siblings and I packed up what remained, I furtively kept looking for those photos—why, I'm not sure. Subconsciously, maybe I thought they could unlock some mysteries about my father and his refusal to mention anything about his war years.

We knew he'd served in World War II and had some connection to the Nazi concentration camps; whenever something would come on TV about Holocaust deniers, he would erupt in anger.

"It happened, I saw it!" he'd yell at the TV, even as his body language said to us: *Don't dare ask.* He never talked about his war experience. Never.

As our work on the house continued, I hadn't found the photos. Then, just as we were almost finished, my brother yelled from up in the attic. He'd discovered the trunk. It was wedged into a corner against the brick chimney, caked with dust.

He opened it and pulled out a Nazi flag. My sister and I burst into tears at the sight of it; what was our father doing with this symbol of horror? My brother closed the lid and hauled the trunk downstairs. The Realtor was pressuring us to get the house cleaned up so the new owners could move in; we were all exhausted, stressed, and rushed. We didn't have time to pause over what was in the trunk; we just hurriedly divvied up the boxes that had been inside it.

I took several home with me to Eugene, Oregon, where I was senior career counselor at the University of Oregon's Career Center. But, burning candles at both ends as usual, I didn't even take time to look at what was inside. Months later, on a rainy October day, I decided it was finally time. I opened one of the boxes. There was a Bronze Star medal and my father's captain's hat. There was a faded enter/exit pass for the Dachau Concentration Camp, a Red Cross armband, and shards of glass, apparently from broken microscope slides.

SUDDENLY, I SAW what jolted me twice: not only hundreds of letters my father had written to my mother, but tucked within them, the photographs I'd seen when I was a little girl.

You are not to look at these—ever!

Never mind that my father had been dead for more than a decade, his disapproval hovered over me like a specter, even if his words were only in my mind. But by now the chill between my father and me had begun to thaw; I was less inclined to allow him to "steal my joy" or, in this case, curb my curiosity. Though I always respected him, he had been a difficult father, a demanding father, but my therapist had encouraged me to make peace with him. I had.

I looked at the photographs—they were sickening—and started reading a few of the letters, handwritten on six-by-nine-inch onion skin paper. As I did so, they began revealing a whole new side to the man, a side I'd never known. After counting, I realized there were more than 300 letters, all written to my mother by a young doctor who was thirty when he'd walked off the gangplank of a ship in Europe, never again to be the same.

The first letter I pulled from an envelope was dated May 8, 1945—the day the war in Europe ended, and nine days after the liberation of Dachau.

"We roared through the gates of Dachau figurative 'minutes' after its liberation while 40,000+ wrecks-of-humanity milled, tore, looted, screamed, cried like depraved beasts which the Nazi SS has made of them," he had written.

He'd been there. He'd seen it. Smelled it. I sobbed as I read on. This letter was his first report on what he'd seen when entering the German concentration camp.

Already emotionally racked, I sifted through the stack. He had written almost every single day, sometimes twice a day. He had delved deep into the horror of war, the spirit of men, and the shame of greed in a way, I later found, that was far different from the more benign letters written by other World War II veterans.

"Perhaps even unprecedented," the *New Republic* magazine would later write about his letters.

My father was a liberator. In early May 1945, it turned out, he was among the first physicians to treat former prisoners at the Dachau Concentration Camp in southern Germany, a place where some 41,500 prisoners were murdered. The physicians' jobs? To establish a medical unit and help save as many former prisoners—many near death—as possible.

Over time, I learned that written accounts of such a place, particularly by doctors, were extremely rare. The incidents he wrote about, and the way he wrote about them, "find no place that I know of in the popular American narrative of World War II and the Holocaust," William

Donahue, a professor of German studies at Duke University's Center for Jewish Studies, told the *New Republic*.

"To most people, this is a very different side of a piece of history we all thought we knew," said historian and author Robert Abzug about my father's letters.

Darker. Starker. Angrier. From the time my father and the 116th Evacuation Hospital arrived in France in November 1944 to the time the unit left Dachau in June 1945, the tenor of his letters darkens like the dusk-to-black transition at day's end. His mood goes from happy-go-lucky and eager-to-be-home to frustration and anger at the horror of it all. Dachau, an ugly exclamation mark to his war experience, sends him over the edge, his once-upbeat letters now gnarled rants spiked with the four-letter words earlier letters didn't have.

Some of my father's letters contained ordinary stuff: grumbles about commanding officers who hid behind their ranks, worries about censors who might delete certain things from his letters, and dreams about rejoining my mother and their newborn son—my brother—back in the states, once the war was over.

But many of my father's letters contained extraordinary stuff, horrific as it was: "Did I 'confess' how PASSIVELY my canteen cup was [taken by a soldier and] used to pour icy river water down SSers' half-naked backs as they stood for hours with a two-arm-up-Heil Hitler before being shot in cold blood?"

In his first letter he wrote:

> Europe's war is over! The emotions in my heart (& the hearts of every 116th Evacer & 127th Evacer) just more tumultuous than millions of others BECAUSE Emily, we are sweating, stinking, "existing" in The Hell-On-Earth-DACHAU! (Let every word of Jan or Dec Readers Digest bore through the middle of your guts—AND MULTIPLY it 100 fold). Dearest, the atrocity reports are true—and more! For over 8 days I've seen-lived-smelled-"existed" it as one of 28 doctors to try correct the medical-horror-component of The-Hell-On-Earth. Bodies starved to 50 pound men piled like rotting cord-wood!

> Huge gas chambers built like shower rooms (as a ruse)! Hangmans scaffolds! Cremating ovens for dead-dying- or still conscious skin-&-bone wrecks of humanity! Stepping high as you walk to work over dead bodies in the street—Storm Troopers (The S.S.), riot prisoners, & man-eating Doberman pinscher dogs—all rotting!

Finally, he more than once implored my mother to spread the word about the Nazis' mass murders, to never forget what happened at Dachau. "All I ask is that you 'instill' it into as many thousands of others as you can—till maybe we can get millions to 'see' it!" he wrote on June 11, 1945.

The photographs were gruesome. One showed what I assumed were two former Dachau prisoners dragging the skeleton-like naked corpse of a man down a hallway with two meat hooks. I covered my mouth with my hand, aghast at the image I'd seen as a child. So this is what my father saw. I had two college degrees and knew my basic history. But knowing that many of these photos were probably taken by my own father gut-punched me like nothing I'd ever experienced. Enough. Overwhelmed, I folded the box shut. I wouldn't look inside again for six years.

Later, in 2015, the *New Republic* magazine and a few newspapers caught wind of my father's letters and, as they sought to dig deeper into my father's past, I allowed myself to do the same. I began getting calls from other media outlets wanting me to tell my father's story, from major universities wanting me to speak, and from national museums that wanted the letters for their collections. I began researching more about the Holocaust and World War II and Dachau. And I began speaking to Holocaust organizations, colleges, public schools, libraries, and others that invited me to tell my father's story.

But I only told the part of his story that he experienced during the war, never the part about what we, as his family, experienced once he'd come home. Until late in my life, I'd never made the connection between the two, the connection between my father's post-war disposition and Dachau. But I've learned that there are two victims of war: those who die and those who don't.

This is a father's story through one daughter's eyes. Nothing more.

Nothing less. It isn't my family's story, isn't my sister's story, isn't my brother's story; in fact, I don't even name them because, as it's been said, "every sibling grows up in a different family." Each sibling's perspective is different based on an array of factors, from when they were born to what they experienced to how they differ from the others. Which is why the only way I can tell my story is to first explain to my father why I'm doing so, with hopes that he would have understood.

A Note to My Father

Dear Dad,

Even though I wasn't born yet when you wrote the letters, I heard you when you told Mom: "Tell the world what happened." I'm doing that in this book. I hope that makes you proud. That's my mission—to tell the story you wanted told. It's my gift to you. It's what you wanted, pleaded for in those letters to Mom in 1945—"to tell thousands so that millions will know what Dachau is—and never forget the name ... ." Even though you had just arrived at Dachau, you were already worried that if people weren't reminded of the horror of this moment in history, it would happen in other places in other times in other circumstances. And I get that.

But what you must understand is that to tell about what you experienced is only part of the story. I must also tell about what you became, in part because of what you experienced. That's not to defy you. It's to honor you for the service you gave our country. I know it might not seem like that; it might seem like I'm, at best, calling you into question, and, at worst, throwing you under the bus. I'm doing neither. I'm doing what you wanted, telling the truth about war. I'm being your voice, by proxy, with the hope that telling the story of our family will unlock the stories of other families for whom the war didn't end with the last gun shot.

As Bruno Bettelheim writes in *Surviving and Other Essays,* "What cannot be talked about cannot be put to rest. And if it is not, the wounds will fester from generation to generation."

I need to share your eyewitness account about the pain of

Dachau—and my own eyewitness account about how different you were from the young doctor who wrote the sweet letters to Mom, and laughed and joked.

You came home from war like a man half-empty. And yet, as an anesthesiologist in Spokane, you gave whatever you had left to give, just as you had in those hospitals in France and Germany. It was the only way you survived the war, by throwing yourself into your job. And people loved you for it—your patients, your nurses, your administrators. I heard the stories, how you, as a devout Episcopalian, would often pray with your patients before you put them under. You were a lot of people's favorite physician. "Doc Wilsey," folks called you.

You nicknamed me 'Clarissey' and you tutored me over Thanksgiving break in 1967 in hopes I'd do well on my human physiology test at the University of Washington. You danced with Mom in the living room to Bing Crosby's "I'll Be Home for Christmas." In your eighty-two years, you were a man of great compassion, a man committed to justice. You helped start a church and led a Boy Scout troop. A Black Belt in judo, you taught my friend who'd been brutally raped how to fight back.

But when you came home from work, Dad, it was as if the "high" of helping others had worn off. You were spent. Your compassion tank was empty. You'd given so much—in the war and on your job after the war—that there was little left for us: Mom and we three kids. It was as if your home became the one place you didn't have to be "on." And when you stopped, when you slowed down, when you weren't on call to thwart the memories, those remembrances of Dachau made you someone you never intended to be. Angry. Abusive. And impossibly demanding; really, giving me a letter-grade for my swim across Wandermere Lake? Dad, that C+ has followed me through life like a shark in the wake of my frantically kicking feet. I spent a lifetime in major universities, served as a dean of students, ultimately directed a career center, and won awards—and yet still struggle with self-doubt.

That, I think, is the quiet, unseen, unspoken legacy of war: the men and women who are changed by it but either don't notice or *do* notice but can't bring themselves to do something about it—men and women who have great effect on others around them. The doctor's life might have exacerbated the challenge for you. Those who help heal others, you know, are often the last ones to reach for help when they hurt themselves. So, they can spend a lifetime living as someone revered (by their communities) and feared (by their families). That was you.

I have struggled greatly in writing this story, which also could be the struggles of someone whose parent came home from Korea, Vietnam, the Persian Gulf, Iraq, or Afghanistan. My initial goal was to simply be your voice regarding the horrors of Dachau and to remind people to "never forget." I never considered sharing our family story. But while researching and talking to mental-health experts, ministers, and the like, I discovered that Dachau was only part of the story. It was the catalyst for a "Part II" that I'd tried hard to pretend didn't exist but did. Ask my therapist. And I came to consider that telling "the rest of the story" might bring healing to others in similar situations—and justify whatever "friendly fire" it might ignite.

When I tell your story around the country, one of the most oft-asked questions is: *What would you say to your father if you had a chance to see him again?* I'd say Thank you for being a light in the darkness. For risking your life while giving care to patients in Dachau medical wards teeming with virulent diseases. For the healing compassion you gave your patients.

I'm hoping you'd approve of me telling the story—the whole story—because it fulfills your motive back then, when you were writing to Mom, to shout from the rooftops what you, yourself, hid deep inside: that good people can sometimes do bad things. That, to use a word you never used early in your letters but came easily for you once you'd been hardened by the inhumanity of war, cruelty, and bigotry: this is the "shit" that happens when people go to war.

What you couldn't know after the war, as you bounced along with the other men in the back of that truck, bound for port and the sail back to America, was that while you had been front-and center in one of the most horrific places in human history, it was if you'd been infected by an emotional version of the typhus that had swept through Dachau after you arrived.

Dad, that wasn't *you*. That's only what you *experienced*. And experiencing it couldn't help but change who you were. How could it not?

I wished I'd known you the way you were before Dachau, when your letters to Mom were lavished with the sweetness of young love. You were humorous, creative, sensitive. But if, in telling your story, we—you and I—can honor the memories of the millions of innocent people who died in camps such as Dachau … if we can tell others whose parents, like you, were never the same when they returned, that they aren't alone … if we can remind the world that the collateral damage of war is far greater than many understand, I will have honored your request. And, I hope, will have made you proud.

Love, Clarissey

PART I
David & Emily

*I will teach you hidden lessons from our past—
stories we have heard and known,
stories our ancestors handed down to us.
We will not hide these truths from our children;
we will tell the next generation*

PSALM **78:2-4**

Chapter 1

There were 2,836,749 reasons why my father loved my mother. Exactly. Or at least that's what he told her once in a letter. That was David Brown Wilsey. He had a scientific, calculated, numeric approach to life, whether the subject was love or war or people or possibilities. After he'd enlisted, he wouldn't tell my mother there was a good chance he'd be able to get leave; instead, he'd break the possibilities into percentages. After a less-than-satisfying day on the rifle range, he wouldn't say he was issued an inferior weapon; he'd say "17 cartridges out of the total 40 jammed."

What's more, he was so medically astute that he couldn't help but allow his "smarts" to find their way into everyday conversations. Once in a letter to Mom, in telling her that he'd lost a hairbrush, he made reference to his "seborrheic dermatitis head."

A fellow doctor with whom my father had practiced put it this way: "David Wilsey never had a simple answer to any question. If you asked him what time it was, he'd give you the history of the clock."

My mother and father's union was an intersecting of love, faith, college, and healthcare. But these were the war years. Nothing was easy, nor was their getting to the altar to be married.

He had been born in Oconomowoc, Wisconsin, a town so small it almost had more "o" letters in its name than people in its populace. The family lived on Lake LaBelle, across the waters from where gangster Al Capone owned a summer cottage.

My father's mother was believed to have been the first female dentist in the state of Wisconsin; Dr. Lillian Gale Wilsey was a woman who refused to be tethered to the cultural expectations suggesting she should be home taking care of kids and baking casseroles. After earning her State of Wisconsin dental license in 1897, she did stay home, but only because that's where she did her dental work. My grandfather owned a haberdashery, more commonly known for people of today as a hat shop.

Lakeside home. Parents with good jobs. It all sounded like a rather cozy life. But it wasn't. My grandfather was horribly mean-tempered and abusive. My grandmother had bouts of deep depression. Dad's sister was a hellion. His brother died at age five.

Amid the turmoil, my father survived by focusing himself on the future—away from this place. When he was ten, he came across his mother's copy of *Gray's Anatomy*. Most boys his age were fascinated by the drawings of women with no clothes on. My father was fascinated by blood vessels, circulatory systems, and the fact that the human body had no fewer than 206 different kinds of bones. He had no idea the human body was so complex. It amazed him. He woke up the next morning and said to himself: *When I grow up, I'm going to be a doctor.* From that day forward he regarded that book as a preacher regarded his Bible; it became his continual companion.

He was just as decisive about his Christian faith, expressing itself through his involvement in the Episcopal Church. He was, as they called it, a "cradle Episcopalian." He loved the ethics of a faith built on "doing unto others what you would have others do unto you," believing in right and wrong. He loved the ritual, the liturgy, the tradition. He loved that he was continuing a family tradition, the Wilseys' Episcopalian ties going back at least three generations.

After his father died suddenly in 1926 of a bleeding ulcer when Dad was twelve, he was enrolled at St. John's Military Academy in Delafield, Wisconsin. It was only eight miles from Oconomowoc but might as well have been across the country for the cultural change it meant for my father. It was there, amid a hierarchy built upon parental wealth and status, that he developed a keen sense of justice. The students at the academy—and to some extent the faculty—quickly delineated a line between haves and have-nots. My father, not having roots in Chicago or Minneapolis but Oconomowoc, was a "have-not." Anytime parents gathered with the school for orientations or social events, his were conspicuously absent.

That said, he made his mark at St. John's. He was lauded by the yearbook for his good looks. More than six feet tall by age thirteen, he emerged as an outstanding athlete, particularly when it came to swimming, which earned him token acceptance by the others.

If his father's death represented the dropping of one shoe, the other clomped down when his mother spiraled into deeper depression and, as was the custom at the time, placed in a mental institution. Dad, at age twelve, already felt like an orphan, something he often shared with us as an adult.

He enrolled at the University of Wisconsin-Madison in 1931, majoring in zoology. His status as an orphan was made official in 1934 when, as a college student, he got the call from the mental institute: his mother, perhaps never recovering from the losses of a husband and son, had taken her life. Although having a married sister in Ohio, my dad was, at age twenty, essentially alone in the world. However, the losses did not deter him. He channeled his grief into his studies, completing the four-year program in three. After graduating from Wisconsin in 1934, he began medical school at UW-Madison with the same resolve.

It's probable that his mother's death left him with little money; nobody was going to pay for his schooling but him. He became the "house boy" at an Episcopal ministry for students, St. Francis House, and involved himself in it. Its chaplain was a young man named Leonard Nelson, whose wife, Clarice, was the house's social secretary. (I would one day be named for her!) When she met David Wilsey, the young doctor-in-the-making, Clarice, twenty-nine, was impressed.

"Emily," she told her twenty-two-year-old sister, a junior at Wisconsin who trusted Clarice implicitly, "there's someone I'd like you to meet."

Ever since she'd been a small girl growing up in Bismarck, North Dakota, Emily Elizabeth Belk had doted on her big sister, at times serving as a parent-appointed "date chaperone" in the backseats of cars belonging to Clarice's boyfriends. The two were strikingly different. Clarice was as confident as Emily was not, as outgoing as Emily was quiet. Emily lived in Clarice's shadow, though never begrudged the inevitable shade Clarice's stature cast. In 1935, when Clarice left Bismarck for Wisconsin and college in Madison with eyes on becoming a journalist, Emily's world withered. She missed her older sister terribly.

She funneled her energy into sports, hiking, tree-climbing, all sorts of pursuits that imbued her with a sort of tomboy image. But seven years later, a year after she graduated from high school, there was only one place for her to attend college: Wisconsin-Madison, where her sister and brother-in-law directed the Episcopal student ministry. She decided to pursue a degree in physical education, even if her tomboy looks had given way to those of a beautiful young woman.

When, in 1935, she met David Wilsey, Emily's world widened in a wonderful way. He was kind, sports-oriented, and, of course, an Episcopalian. He was studying to be a doctor and would graduate from medical school as a member of Alpha Omega Alpha Honor Medical Society. What wasn't to like? David wasn't one to brag, but when the two talked about his love for sports, Emily learned that at St. John's he'd been presented with the "Superman Award" for his sports prowess and academic achievement. He was 6'1" tall and about 175 lbs., lean, trim, strong with brown hair and hazel eyes.

Emily's zest for life drew out a side of him that he'd tucked away in his singular pursuit of becoming a doctor. She had switched majors from physical education to physical therapy, so both had an interest in restoring people to health. They hiked, rode bikes, and studied together. They talked about everything under the sun, including God, the two of them bound, as it were, by a common faith. They dreamed of a future together.

All of which made it more difficult when they went their separate ways.

Chapter 2

In 1939, David and Emily were pulled apart by separate careers and geographic constraints. Four years after they'd started dating, David left for an internship at Kansas City General Hospital. Emily, meanwhile, was offered a rare opportunity to work at the rehabilitation center started, and used, by the president of the United States.

President Franklin Roosevelt, then in his third term as president, had been coming to Warm Springs, Georgia, since 1924 in an attempt to regain strength lost in his lower body because of polio. The place became known as "the Little White House." Knowing the University of Wisconsin's prowess in health and medicine, Roosevelt asked the school to establish a physical therapy department at Warm Springs, a spa town whose mineral springs flow constantly at ninety degrees.

When Emily was chosen as one of two physical therapists from University of Wisconsin, she wasn't about to pass up the opportunity, and David couldn't blame her. After more than eighteen months in Warm Springs, Emily worked briefly at Fitzsimmons General Hospital in Denver. David completed his internship and residency in Kansas City and Cleveland hospitals, then moved west to Elko, Nevada, where he got a job at the Elko Clinic & Hospital.

When the dust settled, the two of them realized there was only one thing missing after they'd each hitched their wagons to professional pursuits: the couple they had once been, the two young people who had once seemed so right together. They rekindled their romance with letters.

They also realized that the winds of war were blowing, threatening winds that only complicated the idea of their winding up together. On December 7, 1941, the Japanese had drawn the United States into war with its unprovoked attack on Pearl Harbor in Hawaii. When it happened, Emily was in Warm Springs, where Roosevelt was, too. In fact, just a few days earlier Roosevelt had been part of a 300-person Thanksgiving dinner that Emily had attended.

Roosevelt's strong handshake impressed her. But, she wrote home, "he looked awfully tired but most courageous. Honestly, one's heart aches for him, he looks so in need of rest." And that was *before* the Japanese invasion.

With Germany's counter-declaration of war on the U.S., American men were fighting in Europe and in the Pacific Theater, against the Japanese. A draft had been in place since 1940 and even though the medical community and college students were among those exempted, such exceptions were being threatened. The draft hadn't produced nearly as many qualified soldiers as expected. Wars in the two theaters was broadening. More troops and doctors were needed.

Some might argue that David Wilsey saw the handwriting on the wall and decided to enlist, with hopes he'd have more say in where he'd wind up serving. But I wonder if my father, inspired by his faith, didn't do the calculations and realize that serving his country was simply the right thing to do. On February 29, 1944—it was a leap year—David Wilsey volunteered for military service as an anesthetist. But not before marrying the woman he loved, Emily Elizabeth Belk, on May 26, 1943, in Bismarck. Within six months, she was pregnant.

My mother followed my father to Boston, where he was stationed at nearby Fort Devens. As part of the 116th Evacuation Hospital, he had been temporarily deployed to Fort Jackson, South Carolina, with a few weeks in Carlisle, Pennsylvania, to learn how to provide medical care for soldiers with war-related injuries.

At Fort Devens' Lovell General Hospital, my brother was born on August 18, 1944—with a "patent ductus arteriosis," or to the lay person, a "hole in the heart." My brother wasn't supposed to make it beyond age six. Because of the complication—routine surgery today—the Red Cross returned my father to Fort Devens. Doctors said there was nothing they could do for the baby now; he would need to get older, and his heart would need to get larger, so a high-risk surgery might be attempted. Because of how hard he'd kicked prior to birth, my parents nicknamed him "Thump" or "Thumper."

In a whirlwind two months of frantic emotions and frenetic travel, my parents tried to establish some sort of foundation for their new roles as parents. It wasn't easy. Dad got sent back to South Carolina, and Mom, they decided, would be best off in Bismarck, with the support of her parents. Once things were semi-settled, Dad rendezvoused with Mom and Thump in Bismarck.

He did what he could to help Emily and Thump get settled. Spent some time with his in-laws. Worried about whether he'd have enough money to get back to South Carolina. Met with a Dr. Brandt Alexis about the possibility of Thump being operated on by Mayo Clinic doctors at the University of Minnesota Medical Center. And washed fifteen diapers, three shirts, and—I have no idea about the context on this item—one kimono.

That my father could be talking about a patent ductus arteriosus operation with a fellow doctor one moment and changing a diaper the next illustrates the sort of man-for-all-seasons guy he was, even if the latter season might have come with a particular stench. He was simply good at many things. Here was a doctor who, while at Fort Jackson, earned "Marksman" level accolades—think Olympic Bronze Medal—during a

5 AM rifle-shooting session. And that was after he'd been out late the previous night at a concert by the Welsh pianist/satirist Alec Templeton.

From the moment my folks were back together, the elephant in the living room, of course, was my father's impending deployment to Europe. He didn't know when or where, specifically, he was going. But suffice it to say that the trip to Bismarck had been one long hello/goodbye. On a multi-flight trip back to Fort Jackson, numerous soldiers had gotten sick, he reported. But my father was only lovesick. "I Love you, I Love you, I Love you!" he wrote to Mom.

Unlike my father's letters, Mom's return letters were not saved; the army wouldn't allow it, though my dad occasionally hid letters—or portions he'd cut out—in his hat. But I have to believe these early months of motherhood were extremely difficult for her, the burden compounded by the sudden loss of her sister, Clarice, who died of a rare liver disease in October 1943. She was only thirty-three.

Without my being able to see Mom's responses, my father's letters lack context; it's like assessing a tennis match while not seeing the return shots. But in these early weeks of him being away, there's a certain glibness to his letters. "Gee! Golly! Dearest, I am not a bit glum or disheartened at all." There's a certain bounce to his step, as if he's excited about this new adventure. And there's a certain sense of levity to his letters, the breadth, depth, and frequency of his humor certainly far beyond what I saw from him in my growing-up years.

The writing itself became part of his "act." He established a nickname for himself, "Wilitzski," what he called a "Scottish-Polish" combination. He created his own off-the-wall language. Whether inspired by his time in the South, it had a hint of hillbilly to it—he'd write "purrtier" instead of "prettier," "confuzin'" for "confusing," and "anyhoo" instead of "anyhow." And he leavened even the most serious themes with lightheartedness.

"I ran in the infiltration course last night. It was … kinda fun. Those heavy machine-gun bullets that were tracers (every 6th or 10th one) sure did look purrty, Ma, as they roared over your head. The sand in your mouth & every square inch of our body 'grated' a little bit. The star shells (to make you 'freeze' motionless) were purrty too, Ma."

Context is important to the levity of his early letters. In the fall of 1944, hundreds of soldiers were dying every day in the European and Pacific theaters. But, stateside, that wasn't the reality. There, as intense as a drill sergeant could make it, the preparation for battle never included a real enemy. And for men in training, there was still time for shows, dinners out, and all sorts of hijinks. For now, my father was either lost in the relative innocence of what must have seemed like either a Boy Scout jamboree or whistling in the dark, knowing that he, too, would soon be swept into the vortex of war.

And, ultimately, his family as well.

Chapter 3

As I sifted through my father's letters in an attempt to understand the man more fully, I determined—in a nod to his love for numbers—that, at least in these final weeks before his ship set sail for Europe, the man was driven by four things: 1) his wife and son, one of whom was rarely mentioned without the other, thus causing me to fold them into a single entity; 2) his faith, which if not dominating his letters, got a consistent mention; 3) his desire to be exceptional at essentially everything he did, including his perseverance to wait in a phone booth line to make a call to his wife; and (4) numbers.

He saw the world like a sportswriter saw a ball game—not only the ebbs and flows but the statistical breakdown of who had done what, as if life could be summed up by a glance at a box score. I should note that of the four motivations, this defined him the least. But to not discuss this quirkiness would be to miss a lighter side to the man that shouldn't be overlooked.

In October 1944, with the 116th Evacuation Hospital now at Camp Kilmer, New Jersey, near New York City, the unit went on an eight-mile training march. My father was probably the only one in the unit who noticed that, although the test was optional for officers, "5 of us out of the 39" went anyway. Of course, he would be one of the five. And, of course, he would notice exactly how many went. If he was going to be an exceptional anesthetist overseas, he rationalized that he should be able to march eight miles as well as the next guy, even though, as he pointed out, he had walked "10+ miles" on the streets of New York City the day before. And "I only spent $2.05 foolishly." Not "a couple of bucks," mind you, but "$2.05."

He was a man of precision. In his line of work, you had to be. Every time he put someone "under," precision was the difference between life and death. He was a man of conscience; he believed we were created by a God who expected people to act with honor in terms of how they treated others. And, of course, he was a man of frugality, which qualifies as a subtopic of the "numbers" category because they almost always involved dollars and cents.

Because he was on his own at such an early age, because his inheritance—if he received one at all—couldn't have been substantial, and because he had seven years of school to pay for, he couldn't afford to waste money. He'd started college in the throes of the Depression. Money was tight, especially for young men trying to put themselves through undergraduate school and medical school.

A week before shipping out, he was stunned to see what some of his fellow officers were shelling out for meals. "Golly! Some officers spend $5.50 to $7.00 for dinner alone—boy!" he wrote. "A guy could really spend dough in N.Y.C. However, a bus ticket from [camp] to NYC costs only $1 round trip & the subways will cost me only 10 cents to 20 cents & the Statue of Liberty boat will be only 35 cents."

He asked Emily to send him a pump to take overseas so his air-mattress wouldn't require so much time blowing up. She did so. In the meantime, though, he learned he wouldn't be allowed to take it. "As soon as I have some money for parcel post I am shipping the tire pump back," he said.

When you're short on money for stamps, you're struggling financially. My father clearly was. The next day, a group of doctors who were out and about came across some great buys in a local store. "It was kinda depressin' to see all the other docs grabbing last minute bargains," he wrote, "& I wasn't able to touch them (yup! Imagine Wilitzski not being able to get in on bargains!?!")

What my father lacked in finances at this point of his life, he made up for with proficiency. He was now thirty. These early years would prove to be the headwaters of a life that would flow with excellence when it came to just about everything he did. He had graduated from medical school as a member of the most prestigious medical honor society in America. He had found, married, and become a co-parent with a woman in whose love he exalted. And as if his third-highest ranking in pistol marksmanship wasn't good enough for him, in late September he scored 87.22%—exactly 1.22 points, he proudly pointed out, above the level for "expert," the "gold medal."

All of this despite having been incubated in a family that was, at best, difficult; at worst, dysfunctional; and at last, simply gone, a sad ending for his parents but, for my father, perhaps a mixed blessing of sorts. Nobody wants to see others suffer from mental illness or die, but in some ways I wonder if, though painful, the deaths of his parents freed my father to reach for all he could be: for God, for himself, and for whomever else would join him on the journey.

In a letter home, he wrote as if speaking specifically to Thump: "Now! I can very happily & pleasurably state that you, Sir, have an Automatic Pistol Sharps Expert's Medal … a Marksman is an average of 62%; a Sharpshooter is an average of 75%; & the highest ranking is an Expert, 86% or higher—your Dad shot FOR you & got a 87.22% to win YOU an Automatic Pistol Expert Medal. Tell your Mother." Not that, as a doctor, my father was expected to engage in combat when he went to war.

The pursuit of proficiency, unchecked, would seem to be a recipe for a lonely, self-absorbed life. But what prevented my father from doing that, at least in these younger years, seemed to be his faith in God. His was neither a shout-it-from-the-rooftop nor a bury-my-light-under-the-bushel sort, but his faith clearly infused him with a perspective that the world was bigger than he was. He saw God not only in the big scheme of things, but in the details, too.

One of his most delicious comments in a letter involved securing some railroad tickets, and came twined with that rare blend of spirituality and his love of numbers: "The P.O. $50 Money Order will be enclosed in a registered letter containing the R.R. tickets tomorrow," he wrote on September 21, 1944. "The good Lord was with us in at least 4 respects regarding that R.R. bedroom, but I'm too tired to describe the 4 respects right now. (P.S. Plane = $94, sending M.O. of $50, I have balance of the $200 for Ft Jck.)"

In the same letter he said he had unpacked in a "2/3rds manner." His constant reference to numbers reflected a man who noticed the nuances of life, the deep grays and light grays among the black and whites. He did not unpack "with a certain lack of vigor" but in a "2/3rds manner."

Even when tired—"I'm dead," he wrote a few paragraphs later—his mind worked like a firefly, darting here, darting there, but always processing. A few days later, he came up with another faith/numbers segue in a letter. First, he made a reference to having attended Trinity Episcopal Church, a structure done in Gothic Revival style that dated back to pre-Civil War days—1847—in Columbia, South Carolina. Then, seemingly out of nowhere, he wrote: "Say, did you know That Numerologist Kelly was once [with] Ringling Bros Barnum-& Bailey?"

On October 5, roughly three weeks before his unit was to ship out, he responded to something Mom apparently wrote about his impending trip to Europe, and war. First, he joked that a "letter a day keeps the psychiatrist away in these potential 'Gang-plank Fever' epidemic zones." Then he promptly pointed out, with his not-infrequent use of CAPITAL LETTERS, that "I HAVE NOT ONE SINGLE BIT OF 'FEVER.' My only (my one & only) feeling is concerning you & [Thumper]—no 'fear,' no lack of courage, & the such that 'infect' so many. I am just positive God has given it to me, this Peace … via the [tradition of the] Episcopal Church!"

His spiritual life was so thoroughly woven into his day-to-day comings and goings that, a few weeks later, he wrote about going to church, about the new chaplain being Methodist, and about how, despite the man not being Episcopalian, the service nevertheless "was worth it cause I found a new Bishop Brent Day Book." And then, in the very next line, with no transitional bridge: "We sent our laundry out today."

God, church, prayer—his spiritual life wasn't some hands-off religiosity reserved for clergy in long robes, but the every-day stuff that wouldn't look out of place right next to, well, yesterday's laundry. The "Day Book" he referred to, not much larger than a deck of cards, was daily inspiration by Charles Henry Brent, the Episcopal church's first missionary bishop to the Philippine Islands. Brent, a New Yorker who had died in 1929 at sixty-six, was revered among many, particularly Episcopalians, as "gallant, daring, and a consecrated soldier and servant of Christ ... ."

It was my father's habit to regularly read this or some other devotional—the Episcopal Church's *Forward Day by Day* was another he favored. Each entry included a verse from Scripture and a nugget of practical advice to incorporate such wisdom into one's day. Amid this calm before the storm, his most urgent prayers were for Emily and Thump. Beyond his updates on life in the military, nothing consumed more in his letters—and, by extension, in his life—than did his expressing love and affection for his wife and newborn son.

He thanked Emily for "making such wonderful babies," encouraged her as she dealt with postpartum blues, and exalted in his being a first-time father. "If all this pistol Expert stuff seems kinda silly/superfluous/much-ado-about-nuthin' to a woman, you just go ask my pal Thump & he will tell you that he is as tickled pink as is his Pop about it all."

The long-distance relationship seemed to be working, though the two had their "moments." One came in regard to a rare phone conversation in which, according to my father, my mother—still deep in grief over the death of Clarice—apparently made some sort of "apology" for his enlisting. It clearly led to a misunderstanding.

> Regarding your 'apologizing' for me being in the Army—please just have NO FEELINGS ABOUT IT

AT ALL—PLEASE!! You say that you don't know what was wrong with you & that you [were] crazy with grief—WELL, PLEASE JUST DON'T THINK ALL THAT EVER AGAIN, DEAREST ... here is the best way (incidentally my way too) about looking at these things—all it is certainly T-R-O-U-B-L-E, this whole maze of things. Well, the Trouble-of-being-apart; the Trouble-of-my-not-being-able-to-help-you-[Thump]; the Trouble-of-war-soldiering in its billion respects; etc; etc are all T-R-O-U-B-L-E to make you & me better people because of it. Dearest, any day or anytime you feel as you did when you wrote that letter of Sept 27, just open Bishop Brents Day Book—there before you in a total whole on Day #23-Day#24 you see in a grand panoramic total The Answer to EVERYTHING IN LIFE THAT ever causes you or me or Thump any heartache/regret/unfathomable thought. Never fail to open that Day Book to that place, my dearest, & may God help you to remember to open the Day Book to split second any such category of feelings arises.

Letters, of course, lend themselves to misinterpretation, as opposed to face-to-face conversation, wherein each party can immediately seek clarification or add the nuance of detail. They also lend themselves, at least in the case of my father, to wandering from this point to that, as if, in being in such a hurry to pour out his myriad thoughts that there was never time to get them organized.

If his letters often flitted from this subject to that—in this case, from phone booths to possible hurt feelings—he was consistent in expressing his affection for his family. War, and preparation for war, comprised a "trial by fire" for hundreds of thousands of relationships. Could marriages and promises of marriages endure all that was to come? As my father settled into the cadence of the military, the men around him reminded him of his fellow freshmen at the University of Wisconsin. Wallets were opened. Photos of wives and girlfriends shared. Promises of fidelity boasted about.

"She'll be there soon as we get back from moppin' up them stinkin' Krauts," some guy would boast.

"If ya'd been smart, ya'd have wrapped up the deal 'fore you left," another would add. "Like me. Married a month now."

My father was optimistic about his promise to my mother, less so about those promises from the men around him. Sure enough, less than two months into the army, he watched as some who'd vowed to stay faithful to "the woman back home" had all but forgotten her name in their pursuit of temporary replacements in bars and at USO dances and shows. Dad's commitment to my mother wasn't arrogant or boastful but was quietly backed up with words to her that suggested a man who was "in it for the long haul."

"Don't think for a single minute, darlin', that I don't know how hard you work for [Thump], and how tired you must be."

He exalted in Thump gaining another "3 1/2 ounces"—not 3 or 4 or "a few"—and was now, at two months, "8 lbs. 4oz!" "Never, never, never forget, dearest, that I have many times said to you (& others too)—I'll put my money on you (your judgment, your thought, your decisions, your care, your everything) any time/day as far as our babies are concerned!!!"

He ended it with a reference to my "Precious Wife & Wonderful Son." It was the last letter he wrote before boarding the ship for Europe, headed for a crucible that he neither fully expected and from which he never fully recovered.

PART II
War

Courage is fear holding on a minute longer.

GEN. GEORGE PATTON
COMMANDER, U.S. SEVENTH AND THIRD ARMIES, WORLD WAR II

Chapter 4

SOUTHERN FRANCE
NOVEMBER 2-27, 1944

About a month before my father's arrival, the autumn rains came to the south of France in torrents. Jeeps spun their tires on once-dirt roads that had become, he wrote, "the gooeyest & heaviest goop you ever ran into." Soldiers in slickers sucked the last life out of soggy cigarettes, water dripping off the curved lips of their helmets. And as if war itself wasn't enough to grouse about, the French prostitutes muttered that the rain was hurting business.

My father arrived as a freshly minted first lieutenant, an anesthetist with the 116th Evacuation Hospital, one of two who would serve the unit. (He wouldn't take the boards to become an anesthesiologist until after the war, so technically was an "anesthetist." His job? To safely support a patient's vital functions during surgery.)

My father had just turned thirty the previous July 11, meaning he would have been slightly older and a little more experienced than a lot of the doctors around him, and at least five to ten years older than most of the GIs whose lives would be in his hands—quite literally.

The 116th disembarked in Marseilles, France, on November 6, 1944, and after a couple of temporary stops, set up in Sarrebourg, about 300 miles east of Paris, close to the German border. German bombers would occasionally roar by, though their payloads were meant for troops, not hospitals, a Geneva Convention edict that its *Luftwaffe* air force usually, but not always, adhered to.

My father was temporarily separated from his 116th Evacuation Hospital, "loaned" to a general hospital whose whereabouts I've been unable to discern, though it was likely in the same general area as Sarrebourg. He arrived when, for the first time since the Normandy invasion five months earlier, Allied troops were at least sniffing victory. They had prevailed despite horrific losses on D-Day June 6 and despite struggling mightily in advancing through Normandy's treacherous hedgerows. Finally, Allied troops had broken the German line on July 25, marking a decisive shift in the European Theater of the war.

On that day, Operation Cobra, a highly orchestrated aerial attack, decimated German troops. When Hitler forbade retreat, those stuck in the narrow "Falaise Gap" became fish-in-a-barrel victims for the Americans; 100,000 German soldiers defied Hitler and surrendered. With the Germans in retreat and the Americans rolling east fast, Allied troops liberated Paris August 25, nearly two months earlier than originally anticipated.

Some 150 miles east of Paris, my father was quartered in a dilapidated hotel that he loathed for its dampness and chill. He found it curious, and a bit creepy, that, less than two months before he arrived, German soldiers had occupied that same space. But units from the U.S. Third Army had liberated the area September 15 as part of the Loraine Campaign. Like the weather, the war in Europe was changing dramatically.

"German units had formed a tough, hard crust behind the invasion beaches, but behind them was a near-vacuum," wrote Albert E. Cowdrey in *Fighting for Life: American Military Medicine in World War II.*

Ten weeks before my father's arrival, U.S. troops had pushed east to the Siegfried Line along Germany's western border. It was a snaking concoction of pillboxes, forts, and bunkers protected by extensive mine fields and "dragon's teeth" anti-tank obstacles, much of the line festooned with tangles of barbed wire. On October 21, Allied troops had captured their first German city: Aachen. It had come with a high price—5,000 casualties, almost as many as Germany had suffered—but represented an immense psychological victory for the Allies. German troops had been backed into their fatherland, and already had lost their first struggle to defend a major city. The momentum had shifted decidedly to the Allied cause; by the time my father arrived in France in early November, the liberators were occupying territory along the border they hadn't planned on reaching until May 1945.

NOT THAT MY father probably would have known more than a sliver of such context; in what was a huge war that fanned out across numerous countries, those fighting it rarely had much context beyond their immediate job—*take this village, go on this reconnaissance mission, save this soldier's life*. What he knew was that France was wet and cold, that the French eschewed toilet paper, and that the enemy was not always "them," but "us." At issue, for now, was only a muffler knit for him by my mother, which had been apparently stolen by a fellow American. But before his tour was over, he would be well-versed in the idea that a man's uniform did not always define his ethics.

"I hunted like mad for half an hour just to be open minded & not go off half-cocked [with] the idea of theft being the only cause for its disappearance," he wrote. "Every time I think of it I just boil!! My #1 obsession for days has been the thievery of these Frenchmen, & now here today I imagine it was an 'inside-job' by one of our own GIs. Tomorrow, I'm going to really put on 'the screws' to do everything possible to run it down."

My father's anger over the loss of his muffler would seem to have been equal parts personal ethics and self-preservation. He held himself, and others, to high standards, a product of his Christian faith that suggested people were to treat others as they would want others to treat them; it bothered him to see soldiers gamble away a "month's salary on one roll of the dice," despite having "wives & babies" back home. In addition, he was cold, having found the heating system in the abandoned hotel balky at best. Wearing a muffler while not on duty would have been great.

All in all, it's fair to say he was GOA—grumpy on arrival. He grew to believe Europe was, in terms of hygiene, pathetically behind the times; he drank coffee not because he liked the taste but because he thought it to be cleaner than water. In a November 2 letter home, his first overseas, he decried not only the "hygiene appliances, which no Frenchman seems much concerned about"—the bidet—but the dampness of his accommodations.

"Once in a blue moon you can feel a feeble thrust of heat trying to push its way through a century-chilled radiator." He often decried the mud, though acknowledged "my mud is minimal compared to that the poor infantry GIs have to deal with." And he worried that he was going to get permanently stuck with the general hospital to which he'd been temporarily assigned. Despite the increased danger, he wanted to be closer to the front lines.

"I hate like Hell to leave my gang/my pals/my swell type of outfit," he wrote on November 7. "Gosh! Dearest, one minute I just cuss & scream—and fret and worry—& the next minute I think that it not only could be a lot worse a 'loan' but I might even be grabbed up by this general hospital as a permanent member & then would always be way behind the front lines. I'd then feel less dynamic/less useful than in an Evacuation Hospital unit."

It's also fair to say that amid such relatively trivial factors, he was starting to understand the seriousness of war. On November 11, he wrote home about having seen his first "traitor" hanged: A French soldier who'd been captured by the Germans and became a collaborator with them. He then returned to France as a spy for Germany. When his betrayal was discovered by the French, wrote my father, "they hot-pokered his eye out & cut his tongue out first."

IN THE LATE-SUMMER months before my father's arrival, the challenge for medical units had been physically keeping pace with, as Cowdrey wrote, "a wild advance that, for a time, seemed likely to end the war before winter." Prior to that, in Normandy, the challenge had been evacuating heavy casualties over short lines. Now, particularly in the southern part of the front where my father was, the challenge was having to evacuate light casualties over long lines. As Allied troops pushed toward Germany—liberating towns along the way to the delight of citizens who honored them with bread, wine, and kisses—the front had grown to 200 miles in length. The longer the front, of course, the greater the challenge of providing the best medical care in the shortest amount of time.

Beyond the length of the line, the weather and geography were changing the war, too. Normandy's century-old hedgerows had proven nearly impossible for tanks to get through; now, in rolling hills, the problem was mud that slowed ground troops— my father said he'd trade it for "eight feet of Bismarck snow"—and clouds that often made aerial sorties, at best, dangerous, and, at worst, impossible.

Meanwhile, near Nancy, to the south of my dad's location, General George Patton's Third Army was building up supplies, ammunition, and much-needed winter clothing. The Third had moved so quickly across France after the breakout from Normandy that fuel supplies couldn't keep pace—and an army couldn't effectively advance without it. Soldiers were enjoying this "forced rest" period, even if there was still sporadic fighting here and there, and casualties were trickling in. My father didn't lack for business on his operating tables, but neither was he overwhelmed. Yet.

Six days after my father arrived, however, Patton awoke at an outpost about a hundred miles to the east, near the town of Metz on the French-German border. The French city had been occupied by the Third Reich since 1940. Unable to sleep because of the rain, he returned to a book written by the German general, Erwin Rommel, *Infantry Attacks*. By chance, he turned to a chapter on a World War I fight of September 1914—in a driving rainstorm. Dammit, he thought, if the Germans could fight in the rain, so could we.

For the last six weeks, U.S. troops had made small-scale attacks on German troops guarding the perimeter. Now Patton was done nibbling on the crust. Within hours, 700 artillery guns opened fire on German troops hunkered down in Metz.

"The discharge," Patton later said, "sounded like the slamming of so many heavy doors in an empty house, while the whole eastern sky glowed and trembled with the flashes."

The attack the Germans feared was coming, had come. And my father was about to be baptized in a bloodier bath of war.

My father's main job—but not only job—was to anesthetize patients for surgery and "wake them up" when the surgery was over. Sounds simple enough. But it wasn't. No two patients were alike; some were thick, some were thin. No two injuries were alike; just when my father thought he'd seen it all, he'd see something different—a soldier who had a grenade explode in his own pocket, a soldier with part of a booby-trap lodged in his lung, a soldier with a bullet in his chest that collapsed his lung, creating a massive infection and, thus, making him "a lousy anesthesia risk." Finally, no two surgeons that my father worked with were alike, though, based on his letters, too many let their well-deserved sense of accomplishment overflow into arrogance.

Beyond that, other variables complicated his job beyond that of an anesthetist back in the states. For starters, he was part of an army on the move and, thus, didn't have access to heavy, difficult-to-transport equipment that would help perform more effective surgeries. Transportation channels were often cut off by the enemy and routes often changed, making it unpredictable as to if, and when, medical supplies would arrive. What's more, medical staffs were terribly thin—war demanded thousands of doctors at the snap of a finger and the supply of stateside doctors was finite, meaning that the standard twelve-hour shift often had to be extended. Beyond generally well-qualified surgeons and nurses, peripheral staff members were—through no fault of their own—woefully inexperienced. Finally, working conditions were less than ideal. (En route from America, he helped with a surgery in which the ship was rocking so severely that "I got down on my knees for stability's sake to give the spinal to a ruptured appendix.")

While the general hospitals were fixed, evac hospitals were on the move. Not as much as field hospitals, which were tented set-ups only a few miles behind the front lines. But evac hospitals, sometimes in tents, hopscotched east across Europe, toward Germany, nevertheless. They might set up in canvas tents for a few weeks, in an old church the next, and in a dilapidated hotel the next. Such structures could be cold, drafty, vulnerable to attack—the Geneva Convention be damned—and so poorly lighted that many doctors arrived for work, day or night, with flashlights in their back pockets.

"French electrical current just absolutely S-T-I-N-K-S," wrote my father. "And, also, it is only 25 kilocycle stuff which makes it flicker, flicker, flicker even worse than a candle." (Leave it to him to quantify, with a number, how bad the light was.)

My father's observation rang true with how an unnamed surgeon described an evac hospital in Cowdrey's *Fighting for Life:* "It is hard for me to draw a picture in words of the dingily lit tent, the grassy-mud floor, the rows of litters filled with their uncomplaining bundles of humanity. Some lie quietly; some groan softly; some lean up on one elbow and talk—almost whisper. There is no sterile white which some might expect to see here. It is all brown, a dirty brown from the doctors to the nurses to the soldiers and wounded."

An anesthetist's window for success was far smaller in 1944 than it is today; too much sodium pentothal and the patient died, not enough and the patient woke up, creating a nightmare that involved pain and, perhaps, panic, choking, a botched surgery, and a lifetime of mental anguish because of the horrid memory the guy would have to endure.

Today, a doctor might have a 10cc-to-50cc margin of safety—and an array of computer-assisted monitors, from electrocardiogram (EKG) monitors to blood-pressure cuffs, to warn of danger. In 1944, in France, my father had more like a 10cc-to-15cc window of safety and, amazingly, used his finger on the patient's pulse to determine whether to increase or decrease the doses.

Soldiers were usually anesthetized with drugs that, today, might seem cruel. Some, such as Cyclopropane, were actually flammable. During World War II, the most common anesthetic was sodium pentothal—known more commonly as "truth serum," a liquid solution (ether) that dripped onto a cotton mask covering the patient's nose until he passed out. Because it produced excellent muscular relaxation, it worked particularly well with men in shock, which, in war, was common.

Back in the states, when a construction worker fell off a platform, he was rushed to a hospital within minutes and could be in surgery within an hour of an accident. In World War II, it wasn't that simple. If a soldier's shoulder was shredded by machine-gun fire, an aid man might drag him to safety and stab him with a shot of morphine, then radio for a litter squad. Depending on the wound, the medic administered plasma, dressed the wound, and filled out an emergency medical tag indicating the man's name, dog-tag serial number, the nature of the wound, and whether he'd been administered morphine.

The battalion aid station litter squad would carry the wounded man back to the aid station, where he was examined for the first time by a medical officer, the battalion surgeon. The surgeon might administer more plasma and morphine and, by ambulance or jeep, send the casualty to the collecting station for transfer to the division clearing station, or field hospital. Here, an emergency surgery might be performed to save the life of a soldier who might die if having to wait to get to a more effective medical post, such as an evac hospital.

Then, and only then, would he be transported to a 450-bed evac hospital, where my father got involved, perhaps ten miles from the nearest clearing station, though still considered part of the combat zone. With my father assisting, surgeons performed acute surgeries.

The chain of evacuation, Cowdrey pointed out in his book, was "deep, complex, and richly developed.... When casualties left the zones of the armies, they were gathered by air and rail holding units and forwarded through two advanced clusters of general hospitals at the battered Belgian city of Liege ... and the French fortress town of Verdun. Rail and air linked those hospitals to the hub of the system at Paris, with its seven general hospitals and convalescent camps, its airfields and train stations and complex railroad yards." Ultimately, a wounded soldier would either be evacuated to England or the U.S., or, when fully recovered, sent back to combat duty.

The kicker in all this for men like my father: No anesthetist in World War II began an open-drop ether procedure and then thumbed through a dog-eared *Reader's Digest*. He had to monitor multiple patients during their surgeries; in this way, he was something like a short-order cook—only if he screwed up, the result was a whole more serious than overcooked eggs. At times, when a glut of wounded arrived, he often was expected to pick up a scalpel himself.

"Surgery was so basic to wartime medicine that all military doctors, regardless of specialty, were officially termed surgeons," wrote Cowdrey in *Fighting for Life*. "Many a wounded man owed his life to a surgeon's actions in just such a moment of crisis." And many a time my father owed his medical accomplishments to an assist from God—or so he wrote.

"God has certainly been helpin' me [in] my anesthesia work," my father wrote on November 16, 1944. "I have written you already about (1) that piece of booby trap in the lung & (2) the decapsulation (releasing) of a whole lung—well today was not 'dramatic' but I did a lumbar parasympathetic nerve block which is all done blindly (by 'feel') with long needles through the back to get around toward the front-lateral body of the vertebrae. Well, I hit the nerve chain and injected novocaine & it relieved this poor guy of the phantom-pain in his amputated leg, & was he happy. He said: 'Hell! doc, that's the first time I have been free of pain in those toes (gone, of course) for 3 weeks, day or night.' P.S. Again, how much do I have to pay you to not tell these N.Y bigshot-surgeons that it is the first one I have ever really done—I have watched a few, but the 'feel' to do it was a God-send.

"It seems that every night I tell you I am poopered-out. I'm sure nothing is wrong with me—it's just the excessive work of a place as big (& yet as under-staffed) as this PLUS the nerve strain of doing serious procedures as well as some new procedures that burn up big amounts of 'nervous-energy.'"

On November 22, Patton's Third Army had secured Metz, but the price they paid wound up on operating tables manned by my father and other doctors. In three weeks, he had gone from wet-behind-the-ear rookie to a seasoned veteran.

He had learned that war was capricious, no respecter of logic, no friend of this side or that. "Would you believe that a hand-grenade could go off in a soldier's pocket and do anything but spread his guts all over the ground? Well, last night we did such a case, & all it did was blow the upper-most edge of the end of his penis off. This all proves one thing that becomes daily more impressed upon one in this war—the most major things can happen in war & mean essentially nothing, while the most minor things can happen & cause death."

This may sound biased—I am, after all, the subject's daughter—but people who knew my father often used the word "brilliant." When sections of his World War II letters referencing medical procedures he performed were shown to a current-day anesthesiologist, the doctor shook his head in amazement.

"This guy knew what he was doing," said Dr. Tom Boubel, who'd also spent time in Spokane as an anesthesiologist, "and he was doing it at a time when anesthesia was still in its horse-and-buggy phase—and in a place, World War II Europe, where all sorts of factors were working against him: weather, lack of qualified support staff, and a waiting-line of patients that probably seemed at times to have no end."

Some people in surgical wards were fresh out of medical school or still hadn't graduated. My father had already spent three years at the Elko Clinic and Hospital, whose doctors, my father-the-numbers-guy pointed out, had done "1,445 operations in its first forty-one days"—or about three dozen a day.

In France, my father was highly in demand. Anesthetists were hard to find, good ones all the harder. There was a reason he'd been on loan to the Third General Hospital and, over Thanksgiving, had filled in with a field hospital. He anesthetized officers and grunts, young soldiers and younger soldiers, Americans and Germans. (According to the Geneva Convention treaty, soldiers wounded in battle were to receive aid by medics, regardless of which side they were on.)

He related better to the enemy soldiers than most doctors because he'd taken German as an undergrad at the University of Wisconsin. He spoke their native language at least well enough to learn that one such wounded man predicted it would take until August 1945 for the Americans to beat the Germans.

"I put a number of Germans under anesthesia, & had one die right under my mask," he wrote on November 27, "BUT so help me I didn't do anything but my best for the guy. He was just too wounded; too poor a surgical-anesthetic candidate; & too major a surgery was needed/attempted. Anyhooo, up here there is a dictum—the more Jerries (Germans) we operate on means the better our boys are doing. It's an absolutely infallible index of how the war is going—an index right in our operating-tents."

Chapter 5

Sarrebourg, France
November 28-December 13, 1944

Though, to my knowledge, the man expressed no particular interest in writing and though his whimsical "anyhoo" style wasn't the stuff of Faulkner or Hemingway, my father excelled at something that every good writer does: he noticed what was going on around him. That could be as trivial as European bathroom habits or as profound as the realization that war changes a man. He hadn't been in France two weeks before writing "war is affecting my mind."

The trivial signs of change weren't particularly alarming: he'd started drinking coffee, was smoking like a chimney (Phillip Morris was his brand), and had grown particularly fond of the word "shit," which might not have been anything new for others but was for him.

He first used it in a letter on December 4 when he told my mother, "For some time now I could have written a 'scorcher-letter' about War. I could really rant with minute details but let me close it out with these generalities: IF, those smug, safe, un-Christian, ulterior-motive shits sitting in Berlin, London, Washington, Moscow, & Chungking could really S-E-E, & S-T-R-U-G-G-L-E to keep alive bodies that are torn to Hell in a thousand different ways by War I absolutely betcha that they would make ways of settling differences on paper instead of on bodies torn to Hell!! Someday I'll give you accurate detailed accounts—but till then just recall your Anatomy & start mentally ripping guts, brains, lungs, mouths, & extremities in all the different ways you can 'visualize' — AND YOU'LL HAVE ABOUT ONE-TENTH THE PICTURE!!"

Wow. That wasn't like the upbeat doc his earlier letters reflected. Among his medical staff, he was the proverbial canary in the coal mine; if he thought things were bad, then things were really bad. But like the drip-drip of an IV, he had already noticed the slow drip-drip-drip of standards, medical and otherwise.

"Each day," he wrote, "we get just a little lower living-level." He decried soldiers working the mail line who would shake packages in search of alcohol, and take it for themselves if believing that to be the case. "Apparently, once they pillage them, they just throw them away if, to their disappointment, they got hair-tonic, shaving lotion, etc., instead of liquor … . It makes we 'tea-totalers' furious & makes the recipient men who are drinkers, very sad."

Then, tempering his attitude, he added: "I am not complaining, I'm just trying to describe a 'phenomenon' that is humorously interesting as one looks back on it. Each day our situation & 'convenience' possibilities become a little less & a little less. Anyhoooo, I've had no trouble or gr[ief] adapting to it—in fact, there is a certain exhilaration about doing it & realizing you can & are doing it."

On the other hand, there was nothing funny about death, and it came so easily, he realized. Said his December 8, 1944, letter:

> Dearest, you don't even have to be near a bullet or a bomb to kill yourself in this organization I am in!! Just do what they ask of you in the line of work [what they ask of you as individual, clamoring, case-grabbing egotistical, unthinking, inconsiderate & "unpanoramic-thinking" individual surgeons] & you'll be dead in just a matter of months from ill health or exhaustion.
>
> The crux of it all is as you already know—an Evac Hosp needs at least 7 anesthetists & we have 2½. 9 anesthetists are preferable & we need [have] two & ½ anesthetists!! These surgeons, on their various specialties, all demand/bicker/connive/heckle & prod you to do them personal favors [(of anesthetizing their case, then & there)] so they can be at ease. So they can be caught up; so they won't have to take their normal civil, decent, turn at having an anesthetists at their disposal!! I'll confess & admit to you as of this moment I have been breaking my damn neck in a foolhardy & reckless way to keep up to their selfish demands—& I have done a good job of it—BUT, Emily, it is not worth it.

All of which lead to his sudden use of "shit" as an expression of frustration. He warned my mother—and her folks, whom he called "Mom" and "Dad"—about his new propensity to use the word, which, for some strange reason, he once wrote on the outside of an envelope—with exclamation marks.

> When I come home I will almost surely embarrass you as well as myself by just 'automatically' saying (way too frequently) the exclamation 'shit! It's bad—yet it's "good." Bad cuz of reasons I need not itemize. "Good" because it has become, over the course of months, a "relieving" expression while all the actual sacrilegious profanity is just filling the air around me. Boy! oh boy! do soldiers ever swear, & I mean swear—every 3rd sentence & sometimes every 3rd word. 99% of it is sacrilegious—swearing which I don't like. I honestly don't imagine I have

said "goddamn," "Jesus Christ," & the like over 3 times in months—but oh boy! do I use the word "shit!"

Yup, dear, horrible 'confession.' I say it real often. In fact, I've embarrassed myself more than once when I forgot nurses were in a room behind me or sumthin'. As I said (above), it's almost "automatic" with me. —Just as "automatic" as it is for these other guys all around me to be saying g—d—, j—c—, g—, etc. Soooo—so be it—— such is the truth. (horrible or otherwise). Guess my rationale is this–if I can stick to just "shit!" while all the rest of the "de-deifying" is literally filling the air around me (nurses too), I'm happy & I'm sure the good Lord is happier too. Sooo, "brace" Mom, & Dad & yourself until I get over it.

IF HE HADN'T lost his sense of humor, he *had* found a growing sense of frustration of being exploited in terms of the hours he was working. I'm not sure when he made the shift from the Third General Hospital to the 116th, but the latter became a functioning hospital on November 30, 1944, and so that may have been when he rejoined the unit that he preferred.

"The Table of Organization calls for 3 anesthetists in an Evac[uation] Hosp—each night from 8PM to 8AM. I do the work of 3 anesthetists (often run 3 cases at once—simultaneously) while a nurse anesthetist does the work of 2 people & an enlisted man we are training does the work of 1½ people. Night after night, this sorta gets ya. Maybe someday Berlin-London-Wash-Moscow ... will stop this thing & reduce the work ratio down to a 1:1 ratio."

By now, the mail from Mom had become his salvation, his port in an increasingly horrific storm. And when it didn't arrive when he thought it should, which was often, he didn't hide his displeasure.

"If we only would get some mail we would all probably be less irritable, defected, & 'hope-less.' Everybody is just about ready to scream because no mail has come through to at least sorta 'take-us-out' of this place for a few wonderful moments while we read words 'n things about something other than guts 'n blood 'n Hell 'n stink … . UNTIL you have the chance to shove this information down the throats of some certain people in the United States of America who never have seen, & never will 'see' what War really is. Even war veterans on the streets or in named-General-Hospitals back home don't really show what's going on over here."

He worried incessantly about my mother and about their now-four-month-old son—and the child's heart defect.

"I'm so God-Thankful that you & Thump are safe 'n sound 'n warm 'n clean —'n W-H-O-L-E."

The last-sentence inference was telling. A month into war, and in contrast with the two people he loved most in the world, he implied that he felt unsafe, cold, dirty, and something less than whole. The next day he again contrasted himself, only this time just to his baby son: "You," he wrote, "are at the start of fine manhood & I am on the ass-end of wrecked-fine-manhood. This is something for the World to think about!"

An advantage my mother and father had when my father left for Europe was their ages; with my father thirty and mother twenty-eight when they parted, they were almost a decade older than many newlyweds who'd been thrown into such circumstances. Ostensibly, they were more mature and better equipped to handle the strain of being apart. However, the flip side was this: they'd hardly had time to establish their relationship before my father entered the service. He had left for Fort Devens near Boston only eight months after they were married. And six months after that, their first child was born. They had little time to establish any sort of rhythm as husband and wife—and no time as parents. My father's involvement could be measured in the week he was home on leave. Beyond the hardship of physical separation, my mother's life revolved around raising a son whose future, because of his heart problem, was uncertain, and my father's life around preparing for war. Huge question marks clouded their futures.

Amid such, the sentiments expressed in letters home became something of an artificial attachment that could look and feel good on paper but weren't tested by any sort of practical experience. The letters gave my father a place to express himself, to vent, to pontificate about the injustices of everything from war to Naziism to stone-hearted commanding officers. However, writing about one's ideals and living out those ideals can be two different things.

Because my mother's letters to him couldn't be saved, it is more difficult to suggest what writing letters—or receiving letters from my father—meant to her. I'd surmise it was a mixed bag, a blend of encouragement, affirmation, and levity from my father that probably brightened what might have been days that leaned toward living-with-her-parents boredom and single-mom frustration. But those same letters might have also filled her with apprehension, uncertainty, and a sense of the chasm that was deepening between the two of them because their lives were consumed by two vastly different experiences—hers on raising a new life, his on being confronted by daily death.

She must have wondered if the life she'd dreamed of with my father would ever resume after the war-caused disconnection. She must have had fleeting thoughts about whether the man who left for Europe in October 1944 would be the same man who'd return. Then again, fortified by the American optimism of the times—and the innocence of not knowing better—she may well have expected a life that, if not bliss, would be as beautiful as my father's letters promised.

By now, mid-December, days were getting shorter, the weather colder. Snow began mixing with, or replacing, rain. At times, plastic packets of replacement plasma had to be tucked next to truck radiators to keep them from freezing.

"Surgical tents sagged under accumulations of snow, and the bellies of the wounded steamed when surgeons cut them open," wrote Cowdrey in *Fighting for Life*.

It had been nearly six months since the D-Day landings and, after a handful of moves, the 116th Evacuation Hospital remained in Sarrebourg, France. As nurses cut the clothes off wounded soldiers, surgeons were no longer surprised to find young men with incisions in their bodies from Normandy—now back for seconds, sometimes even thirds.

Each night, my father finished his shift and, flashlight in hand, wrote home. Gone were the days of taking potshots at French men for sleeping in the nude or commenting on how much he was enjoying the muffler mom had knit him—and which, without explanation in his letters, had been reclaimed or found. Instead, he kept chastising the world leaders who'd gotten everyone into this mess—and his army superiors who were keeping him working at a breakneck pace.

"As of this moment I vow to you that I will no longer keep up this pace of doing 3 (& sometimes 4) anesthetists' work just to please & keep happy such selfish unthinking men! Naturally, I think of our wounded boys—but darlin', how can God, or Commanding Officers, or you, or anyone condemn me for not going beyond the full hard sincere work of one-anesthetist man each day."

And yet he did. He kept going, day after gruesome day.

"You know my personality (how I go intensely at work) & what I feel about 'doing' for our-boys, & as 'your-agent' in this war—Em! I tell you I just must do what I've vowed and said above or I'll never get back to you & [Thump]. One thing that makes it all 'hurt' so is that one nurse-anesthetist, for example, goes glibly & unthinkingly off to Paris on a 4 day leave when she knows what the situation is. Lord!"

On December 12, his vocabulary expanded to include "Damitohell," because mail service was slow. By now, words from his beloved Emily—"Em" as he often called her—had become his lifeline, seemingly the one thing that could right the wrongs.

He told her that the last letter he'd gotten from her was one in which she'd told him "a boy from Bismarck had 'got-it' in Holland & another who 'got-it' in Italy." Then came a dark twist: "Emily, have you any idea just how fortunate those boys were?!?! —to 'get-it' outright!! This sounds odd doesn't it? —well just climb inside the pocket of an Evac. Hosp. doctor. Quote me all over Bismarck too—it may help some mothers & wives. (I'll omit details.)"

Reading such letters made me hurt for him, but helped me understand what it must have been like for my father, and how seeing a bloody parade of wounded—and, at times, dying—soldiers every day was already wearing on him. But amid the dozens of letters regarding my father's first few weeks in France, the one that touched me deepest wasn't one he had written but one he had received—and found a way to keep. It was from a man named Bill Faber, who my father had apparently chosen to be a godparent to Thump. He inferred he was older than my father, and that he, too, was a doctor. They were roommates somewhere along the line—medical school or perhaps during a residency.

"Was so glad to hear that you had enough confidence in my ability as a Christian to name me a sponsor to your beloved son, and I wish to thank you

the honor," he wrote shortly after Dad embarked on the ship for Europe. "I shall do all I can do to see that I am worthy of my duty, you can be sure."

What struck me about the letter was its depth, sincerity, and respect. This was no obligatory "how's the weather?" note written by a casual buddy, but a letter by a close friend, a letter that underscored that the roots of my father's relationships ran deep into the ground of his experiences.

Dr. Faber told my father that Emily should feel free to call on him if she needed help with anything, and ended the letter by casting a look to a day when the war would be over.

"In spite of the year since we were roommates, I still feel that certain paternal interest in your welfare which I had at the time—and an affection which the years have juried to be the basis for an enduring friendship. I hope when the war is over you will receive all the happiness to which your long efforts have entitled you. Be good. Bill Faber."

When I'd finished the letter, the part that put a lump in my throat was the latter—the reference to my father receiving the post-war happiness he deserved. After what the man would go through in the war, my father did seem entitled to such.

On a professional level, I think he would find it. But on other levels, I will always wonder if instead of the war being the reason my father "deserved" happiness, it was the reason that, when he came home, he could never quite find it.

HIS MOOD RALLIED on December 13 when casualties were inexplicably light. "You won't believe it—& I still can't believe it!—that I'm starting your daily letter up here in the operating room during duty hours! Yup, today has just gone kerplop in the number of casualties—during my 12 hours today there will have been only about 12 to 14 cases in the O.R.—which is just unbelievable. Anyhooo, we're awfully glad as it means just what it means—fewer of our boys are getting nailed."

What he didn't know—what even the top U.S. military brass didn't know—was that, as he was penning those hopeful words, fifty miles to the north one thousand German tanks were clanking methodically through the snow from points east toward the Ardennes Forest, near Bastogne. The tanks were flanked by 200,000 troops. They were part of Adolf Hitler's do-or-die counteroffensive. History would remember it as the Battle of the Bulge.

It would be the largest and bloodiest single battle fought by the United States in World War II.

Chapter 6

Sarrebourg, France
December 16, 1944 to March 20, 1945

The biggest anomaly of the Battle of the Bulge was the snow. In December, it fell gently in the Ardennes Forest and blanketed nearby villages, farms, and rolling hills with the appearance of whipped cream. The snow painted the Belgian landscape with the proverbial "Christmas card" look, bringing a throat-lump to GIs for whom this time of year only intensified their thoughts of home—and how faraway it now seemed. But that same snow was often marred with blood.

The wintry stillness could, in an instant, be shattered by the pounding of shells from a German 88mm gun. The silent forest could be rocked with the sound of freight trains as explosions splintered trees.

And the pure white snow was soon tainted with the crimson of dead and wounded soldiers, some of whom would later stare up at my father, their eyes pleading for either a miracle or a quick death to rid them of the agony of going home without a leg—or worse. More than once he wrote of how, in war, dying was easier than living.

"SONOFABITCH!" he wrote. "It's just awful what this war does to bodies, educational memories, property, minds, & lives."

In late December, one soldier, a fresh-off-the-boat replacement in the 2nd Ranger Battalion, was brought into an aid station, wide-eyed and speechless. He'd been standing within a few feet of a buddy when the man's head had been blown off.

My father, of course, did not witness his patients at the time they were wounded; he only saw them hours later. Though he and front-line soldiers saw two different wars—the soldier saw the cause, my father the effect—what grated on him was the non-ending nature of it all; as soon as one man had been operated on, another was suddenly *there,* and the pattern repeated, twelve-plus hours every day, seven days a week.

"We are all getting pretty 'dull' & 'jangelly' [sic] by the incessantness of it all here ..." he wrote.

On December 16, 1944, the Germans launched the surprise counterattack on the U.S. Army. It stretched across a seventy-five mile swath of dense, snow-covered forests and rolling farmland along the Belgian-German-Luxembourg border. Though running low on fuel, the Germans had deeply dented the U.S.'s line at Bastogne, Belgium. At the time, long before history referred to it otherwise, my father called it the "Belgian-Bulge."

Within a week, the surprise counteroffensive had encircled the Americans, leaving the 101st Airborne—the focus of Stephen Ambrose's *Band of Brothers* book—as the proverbial "hole in the doughnut." The attack had the potential to reverse the Allied advantage in Europe. Since the breakout in Normandy in July, the Germans had been in retreat to their homeland. Even if Adolf Hitler's favor was waning with some of his officers—an assassination attempt by them had only recently failed—his surprise counterattack was enjoying early success. Its goal was to cut west through those Allied lines, split British forces from American forces, and allow German troops to capture Antwerp, Belgium, a key Allied port for supplies.

Now that the Germans had surrounded four Allied armies, Hitler believed the enemy might be quickly dispatched of; the Germans enjoyed a three-to-one advantage in men, the Americans having assumed the war in Europe was all but won and been caught off guard.

If Antwerp was the kingpin in northern Belgium, Bastogne was the same thing in the south. Seven roads crossed through the southeastern Belgium town, making it a strategic choke point from which Hitler wanted to flush every American soldier. By December 22 he was so confident of victory that he believed Germany could win the war in Europe without even taking Bastogne, that the huge German advantage in numbers could force a U.S. surrender.

Meanwhile, the Americans not only had been taken by surprise by the Germans, they had been negligent in preparing for winter fighting, period. The winter of 1944-45 would prove to be the coldest and wettest that western Europe had experienced in thirty years. But months earlier, when U.S. troops were awaiting supplies, the priority had been for gasoline and ammunition; there was hope that the Germans might surrender before winter even began.

When learning of the Germans' surprise attack, U.S. Army General Dwight D. Eisenhower decided to defend Bastogne at all costs. He issued an order for units on the south and north of the front line to surge toward Bastogne to fortify the troops that were holding out, if only barely.

THE 116TH EVAC Hospital remained in Sarrebourg, which was some 100 miles southeast of Bastogne, Belgium, the epicenter of Bulge fighting. As Christmas neared, my father was flanking surgeons who were up to their elbows in the blood of men wounded, or dying, from injuries suffered in the Battle of the Bulge. That would go on for five weeks.

In its first forty-four days of existence—November 30 to January 13, 1945—the 116th Evacuation Hospital would handle 3,900 casualties. Most of those came after the surprise German attack on December 16, meaning my father's unit, at times, was averaging nearly 150 patients a day. A first lieutenant nurse from the 116th, Thelma DeWitt, later told a U.S. newspaper reporter that at its peak, during the Bulge, the unit handled ten times as many in *a single twenty-four-hour period.* For the 116th, things had gone from bad to worse.

"The winter of 1944-45 was a time not so much of a single crisis as of an irregular barrage of crises, among which the medics dodged like people caught in a hailstorm," wrote Cowdrey.

In a letter to my father, my mother had said it seemed surreal having her husband mixed up in the ugliness of war. His response? "I know exactly what you are saying & I agree—YET, in another sense/phase, it is so real—so rock-bottom and dastardly real when you live it 7-days-a-week. Ya know—this 7-days-a-week is an aspect of War that nobody realizes until they live it. Lordy! How you'd give anything for a half day off from Destruction! After a while this 7-days-a-week just bores into the middle of you."

If my father was overwhelmed by the war, I was overwhelmed by his letters. His frustration. His exhaustion. His glass-half-full nature already battered by a sense of hopelessness. I could almost feel his pain, the cold, the despair as he tried to save mutilated body after mutilated body.

As the winter deepened, the 116th was packed not only with soldiers wounded by the enemy, but soldiers chilled by winter—and their minds numbed by war. GI field shoes weren't waterproof; trench foot was felling soldiers by the thousands. Because of prolonged exposure to the cold and wet, their feet had become numb. Their feet swelled, developed blisters, and grew fungal infections. It got so bad for some that they developed gangrene, and had to have one or both feet amputated. Between November 1944 and April 1945, 45,000 American soldiers were hospitalized for this reason alone; for every ten men evacuated by the Third Army, six of those men had injuries related to cold, wet feet. Some were so desperate they wrapped their boots in burlap.

The other type of injury that caught medical personnel off guard was shock. Psychological wounds. Soldiers who had seen, or experienced, too much. By war's end, more than 150,000 men would be treated for such; for every three men killed or wounded, one was hospitalized for combat exhaustion. Some took their own lives or tried. Others intentionally shot themselves in the foot so they'd be unable to keep fighting—and might get a "ticket home."

A dozen evac hospitals were fed soldiers from the Bulge. My father's anesthesia unit was working at seven operating tables. If each of those tables represented a spoke on a wheel, my father found himself in the hub, going from table to table as necessary. To make more beds available for the wounded, a dozen hospital trains were running between Liege, Belgium, and Paris, carrying patients to already-crowded hospitals. At times, trains arriving in Paris had to wait on sidetracks for a day or more before they could be unloaded. Hospitals set up beds in hallways. Some patients were put in hotels. What exacerbated the overflow problems were wounded German prisoners-of-war who doctors like my father were also treating; unlike U.S. medical establishments, the Germans had no penicillin and many of their wounded soldiers suffered serious infections because of it.

The Americans' policy in the European Theater of Operation was that if a patient needed six months or more hospitalization, he would be sent to the states. But, during the Bulge, with beds so scarce, that was shortened to four months.

As GERMAN MECHANIZED units broke through American lines in places, some medical units were captured and sent into Germany as prisoners; on December 19, the 326th Airborne Medical Company of the 101st Airborne Division's Combat Surgical Hospital was such a unit. In the attack, a number of medical vehicles carrying the wounded caught fire. Doctors died.

There is no evidence in my father's letters to suggest that the 116th ever experienced such danger. There *is* evidence that the greater danger—at least from my father's perspective—wasn't the Germans, the Jerries, the Krauts, whatever the men called their enemy. The greatest danger was war itself—and what it did to a man's mind, body, and soul.

"We aren't complaining," he wrote. "It's just the incessantness of War just kinda eats at ya/wears ya-down after a while."

At Christmas, my father enjoyed a brief respite from it all. Unlike many of the GIs, whose packages from home were confiscated and destroyed lest they fall into enemy hands and give the Germans an advantage, my father got a present from Emily's parents on December 22.

"Thanks a hundred million!" he wrote. "Ho! Ho!

The 116th handed out candy bars, peanuts, soap, three cigars, and two bottles of beer to each member of the hospital. "Of course we had to pay 96 Frances to get it—but even so it is a 'gift' & a Christmas gift." My father was pleased to be able to attend an Episcopal "Xmas Eucharist" on Christmas night to satisfy a spiritual side of him that had gotten little nourishment. But based on the number of words he wrote about it, the coup de grace of Christmas 1944 was the 116th decorating a tree after cajoling a French civilian to cut one down for them. He described the making of the decorations in delicious detail:

> We'll start at the top-star of the #1 picture that's an inside (shiny) of a plasma can rolled out flat & then cut with the hospital engineers' tin shears. Next you see a balloon-like ornament—those dozens of Xmas-balloons are cut-off fingers of rubber gloves blown up by mouth …. Then you dip these balloons in 10-12 different "dyes" made from laboratory & pharmacy chemicals; or you make a 'mush' of plaster of paris & 'frost' (like a cake) the balloons with pure white or dye-impregnated plaster of paris.
>
> You also paint all appropriate & ingenious colors onto dyed or undyed balloons with a throat swab as your 'artist's-brush.' Now take a tongue blade. Use natural color; total dyeing; or staggered-dying of the whole blade—then diagonally wind adhesive tape (thus the barber-pole effect) & either make it more contrastingly white with p. of paris, or dye it in 10-12 different colors. On #2 you see nearest my head, spiral-like thin structures—that's brilliant silvery plasma or medicine cans cut into long-thin-twisted-"snakes" (really pretty!) Cotton-'snow' bedecks all over. The stick candy dug out of "Boxes From Home" is an adjuvant. See the one of the many cotton

'snow-men'.

His color, his adornments, are all 'ingenuities, including the mystery 'Who Stole The Cap to the Argyrol Bottle'—until you find it being used as Mr. Snowman's cap. Someplace—somebody dug up … "icicles" of tin-foil like material; maybe, brain surgeons foil—no one will ever know!

Good ol' homey-Xmas-ingenuity-by-A M E R I C A N S! Next get all your 'loose' rations you've h-o-a-r-d-e-d, & bring 'em for Xmas presents to each other and for the French civilians who work by your side. You have no nice wrappings, so you turn your back while one of your roommates digs into your own precious [un-opened!] packages from home to unwrap the pretty papers & findings so as to put them on the "Little-Things" pooled for Frenchmen or your fellow workers. The fattest-shortest doctor will act as Santa the next morning, of course. Now how ya gonna light it? Take black-out candles & whittle them into 'Xmas-candles.' Get a belly-surgeon's flood-light-bulb & use that in a concealed manner for spot-lighting/'showing-off' the tree just like on Chicago's Gold-Coast. When you're done you step back & look—yes, Em & [Thump], you look impartially & you & all visitors agree that it is A-C-T-U-A-L-L-Y B-E-A-U-T-I-F-U-L! … Sooo, My Precious Ones, that is very briefly how Beauty and Xmas Come Out Of Nothing in a wrecked, rotten, stinking, sordid Europe.

That my father spent so much time describing the intricate details of this tree suggested just how coveted such small moments were amid war, a much-needed respite, a distraction, a rare link to home. On a broader scale, Christmas Day brought hope to the Allies on the battle front. After their commander rejected the German demand to surrender, Allied troops battled back. The skies cleared; planes were able to get back in the air. British and American bombing raids paralyzed a German transportation system trying desperately to replenish its armies with fuel.

At Eisenhower's request, Patton directed three of his divisions in eastern France, not far from the 116th, to make a 90-degree turn and highball north. They hoped to stem the enemy advance, and relieve the 101st Airborne, which was trying desperately to keep the Germans from taking Bastogne. Despite logistical nightmares, bitter weather, and icy roads, an entire corps, about 60,000 men, arrived at the southern flank of the Bulge. On Christmas Day Patton's Third Army broke through German lines.

My father got the leftovers—on his operating table. Every victory was costly; by the end of January, the 47th Infantry Regiment would lose well over 100% of its *original* strength to battle casualties—men either killed, wounded, missing, or taken prisoner, even as replacement soldiers tried to shore up the losses. (The unit increased in size with the addition of men, meaning a unit could lose its original strength and still have soldiers to fight.) Other units suffered similar losses. Along the seventy-five-mile front, 12,652 Germans and 19,000 Americans would ultimately die, along with more than 3,000 civilians, according to *Warfare and Armed Conflict: A Statistical Encyclopedia*. Some 38,600 Germans and 47,493 Americans would be wounded,. And more than 50,000 soldiers on both sides would simply never be found: buried in rubble, ground into the earth by tank tracks, obliterated by shells, lost in plane crashes, disappearing in ways that only war can imagine.

Only a week into the new year, 1945, my father was as low as he'd been high just a short time before. "Things have been pretty miserable/rotten/disheartening in all phases of daily life here the past 4-6 days & each day things seem worse," he wrote on January 7 1945. "No letter had come for 4 (or 5 or 6) days & that on top of everything else had me (& most everybody else, too) really at the lowest ebb we've been since arriving overseas.

"The #1 keynote is of course the un-human, supra-human, unbelievable amount of work that has been thrown at us this past week. You can stand it ('take it') for a while—then it just begins to 'eat' you right through the middle. The more it 'eats' & the deeper it 'eats,' the more and more and more piles on you. You both 'scream,' 'cry', and 'beg' for other medical units to come & help & they never come—so there is just no stopping/no let up. Finally you almost go nuts!

"Emily, when we think of the doctors sitting on their dead asses back in army hospitals we just can't help but feel a combined hate/disgust! (I know you'll just say I'm tired, upset, etc.—that's not it at all as TRUTH IS TRUTH—I just never told you before.")

It wasn't just the numbers that bothered him, either. It was the attitudes. If my father was all about precision and integrity and compassion for others, he was unable to stay silent when he saw others not only neglecting such things, but spitting in the face of such standards.

"I told you once before about these narrow-minded, unpanoramic-thinking, case-grabbing, egotistical, inconsiderate, unthinking surgeons—don't think for a moment they have changed much. As I've written—there is just a limited (understaffed) anesthesia (personnel and material) in any Evac Hospital yet they grab-'scrounge'-bicker-&-'weedle' against each other & often against the anesthetist because he doesn't do them personal ('pet') favors .... Emily, it nearly drives a person insane. Lord knows we're always busy enough; 'heckled' enough; 'run ragged' enough by just normal things—then add this dastardly 'surgeon-element' on top of it & you've got a picture that just defies written description."

If he had a higher rank, he pointed out, he might be able to effect some change, but that wasn't likely to happen. As a first lieutenant, he'd gotten on the wrong side of a major in charge of promotions—because "I can 'see right-through' him. He knows it, and that's why he hates me so." Meanwhile, another man poised for a promotion would, he predicted, "use his ass-kissing 'inside track' to the Commanding Officer to 'spike' my early captaincy ... ."

Despite overwork, operating-room politics, increasing enemy threats, a spike in the number of wounded soldiers, and the bitter cold, my father clung to a certain survivor's mode that kept him going. Part of it was his faith; he believed it was God's will that he was there for a reason, even if that reason could grow fuzzy amid the horror and hopelessness. Although his attitude ebbed and flowed, sometimes to dangerously bitter degrees, he resisted letting his actions follow suit. He never defied that major. He never chided the "ass-kissing man" eager for the captaincy my father thought he deserved. He never gave less than his best to a patient, even if the man was German. In a January 8 letter, he spoke of doing his best even when he had Nazi soldiers on his table.

"Do you honestly suppose, dear, that Nazi (anesthesia) doctors would have 'gone out of their way' & worked hard to save 3 fast-dying American boys on the operating room table, who would otherwise outright [have] died under his left hand holding the mask?! Nazis would have died today—there are 5 or 6 others in past whom I did similarly for. All I do know—GOD IS OBSERVING!" My father was diligent about doing all he could to save every patient, regardless of the color of his uniform.

Part of it was the emotional oomph he got from Emily's letters; they reminded him of another, better, world—a world that was warm, cozy, comfortable, and filled with love, not the hateful stuff of war. "Oh, precious," he wrote, "your letters are such lovely things. So nice, so sweet, so kind, so warm, so 'purr'-creating! The way you tell me about Thump just does so much that I darn near cry. It's an exalting cry, not a sad one. I feel so ashamed when I received 3 like today after having written 'bitching' letters recently."

Finally, part of it was something new—a gradual but definite shift to "coming out of his shell" a bit and interacting with others more. To some degree, I think my father had always been something of a loner; dating back to prep school, he was never that "in" kid who'd come from money. He scratched and clawed for everything. That didn't make him uppity, but I do sense that he was that person who could let his penchant for perfectionism keep people at arm's length. His respect for protocols and procedures—quite necessary as an anesthetist—might have left him slightly awkward in terms of just "being one of the guys."

He saw the war ending, but not necessarily soon. "Maybe (we and Russians) can whip these sonofabitchin' Nazis before August 1945!" he wrote.

As much as he detested the enemy, he also respected this enemy. "The Nazi IS the best fighting Thing (not human) in the world BECAUSE he has it innate & inbred & instilled in him. Ask any soldier who has fought them all ... We are superior in physique, equipment, material, courage & GOD'S HELP—but not in F-I-G-H-T-I-N-G."

On January 17, 1945, with the Battle of the Bulge winding down and troops moving east, he wrote Emily that he was going to do his "first socializing" since arriving in Europe nearly four months earlier. A "Major Blocksom," from the field hospital he'd briefly been loaned out to over Thanksgiving, arrived as a loaned-out surgeon. Dad liked him. "He's not only a 'good Joe' but an absolutely brilliant surgeon," he wrote. "I was never so satisfied or enthusiastic or happy as when I was with Major Blocksom's team."

Blocksom loved his scotch. After dinner, he invited David for a few drinks. "Sooo, an hour from now I should be having a good time (my first 'time')," he wrote.

He also developed a friendship with Corp. Chet Derbin, a friendship that had begun when Derbin—a prankster—had given my father a "hot-foot": stuck a match into his shoe when he wasn't paying attention and lit it. Derbin was only nineteen years old, short, Polish, a kid from the coal mines of Scranton, Pennsylvania. And yet eager to learn anesthesia from my father.

"He is one of the most personable individuals in the world. On top of everything else the kid has an innate intelligence & natural scientific ability. I've taught him to be an anesthetist & he is damned good. He can pass an intratracheal anesthesia tube about as good as I can; he gives a good pentothal, ether & Heidbrink-machine anesthetic. On top of it all, he has such good horse-sense in anesthesia-emergencies. I now finally can turn my back on the other nurse (recently trained) anesthetists & others with peace of mind cuz ol' Derbin can & would handle an emergency well."

The two developed great mutual respect for each other. Dad liked Derbin because of his enthusiasm, his talent, and his fun-loving nature—not my father's strong suit. "And he thinks I'm a 'God.' I have him 99 percent convinced to become a doctor."

Each man brought out something the other didn't have: Derbin's fun-loving nature lightened up my dad, and his proficiency at jui-jitsu inspired the latent athleticism that the medical profession had doused in my dad. Meanwhile, my father mentored, and inspired, Derbin to consider going from the coal mines to the operating room.

"If it weren't for little ol' Chet my life would be pretty dull & drab,"

Dad wrote.

A third doctor who worked with them was a young French woman, Jacqueline Labesse, whose goodbye letter to my father, when she was ordered elsewhere, was so precious in her limited understanding of English that my father copied it and sent it home: It said, in part, "I have been very sad to not say you adieu before my starting; but I have not dare to awake you because thought you are very tired with the working of the night. I was very sad to set out without your photography."

She apparently wished to take a photo of him so snapped one of him sleeping to "go with my photographies of my others friends of the 116th hospital. But surely I shall not forget never the remembrance of you who were with me the best of teachers and more than good and more than pretty. I hope you understand my bad explaining … Give me the permission to thank you very sincerely for all everything you have done for me. Give too a strong fisticuff to Chester [Chet Derbin] for me, and for you my friendly shake-hand."

GERMANY WAS BEATEN—NOT that Hitler was about to surrender. Instead, in a desperate attempt to stop the Allied advance, he had forced all males between the ages of sixteen and sixty to take up arms. They were to bring their own clothes, blankets, and backpacks. And if they didn't? The Gestapo would show up to make sure that wasn't the case. The Allied advance quickened. The age of German soldiers dipped even lower, to fourteen and fifteen. Even girls were called up.

My father's anger raged—not just at Hitler but at the thought of this god-awful war extending to Japan, which had the potential to be a worse blood bath than Europe.

> Isn't it unbelievable what fools those Nazis can be? They are hemmed, "bottled," beaten, & progressively being annihilated—yet they won't give up BECAUSE— it is the proven component in Totalitarianism that the more you can drag down & kill your adversary while you are "dying," the sooner & better you can again through stealth & deceit arise against him. Here the "Big Three" Conference is over; they know the absolute/irreversible

> "score"; yet they will not stop this wrecking & bloodshed—just because they know they can arise again! it's going to take a powerful-lot-o'-livin' to beat this Totalitarianism "game" in your & my lifetime. Japan, with its CBI Theater, which we must fight "plays-the-cards" the same way. Can you even dream (as I have dreamed) what a frontal assault on Japan land will be like?!— a holocaust if there ever was one!

His spleen wasn't fully vented.

> Truth and totalitarianism just cannot coexist. One of the two has to die. For several hundred millions, totalitarianism did not die-so TRUTH had to. And even the democracies have had to play the same way at times to help fight fire with fire. Even in the Army, bad results/happenings have innocently happened because of the democracies necessity for ignoring/supressing the TRUTH. So it results in my sitting in this world just screaming Shhhhhhiiiiiiiiiiiiiiiiiitttttt!

As tough as my father was on the Nazis, he blamed post-World War I England for baiting Germany into World War II. "Honest, Em," he wrote, "it's true on at least a percentage basis … so much of so many things in this world-mess are 51% (up to) 100% due to England's imperialistic policy/actions for decades."

But he also saw enemies within—and with good reason. He was emotionally parched from a commanding officer so intent on playing the tough guy that he failed to realize that good leaders pat an occasional back and give their "underlings" a rest.

On a handful of occasions, my father told Emily his getting a promotion had never been about any bragging rights of his own. On January 17 he wrote: "A very sweeping summary, however, is this—I WANT MONEY—MORE MONEY—for you & Thump; which part-and-parcel means Captaincy."

He was considering asking for a transfer to an auxiliary group. "To stay with this 116th might keep me always a 1st Lieutenant."

In my father's eyes, his C.O. had almost as much "gestapo" in him as the Nazis. He "saw through" a man who hid his insecurities with bravado. My father had refused to kiss up to the man, his forthrightness obviously worrisome to the guy. He was worried, frankly, that the man so hated him that he not only wouldn't promote my father, but he might find ways to punish him. That he might, as so many insecure leaders do, give my father just the opposite of what he wanted. And apparently he wasn't the only one in the 116th worried about this

"We all live in fear of what is called 'Army-spite'—a C.O., in a 'gestapo-like' manner, having someone who speaks openly, truthfully, sent to some Pacific island, Alaskan, etc. outpost for duty for years—they can do it Em; they do do it, Em; & don't ever think they don't. [In] this war it is even more possible & tragic as for years the world will be an armed-camp & doctors just must be on remote islands, etc., etc. for years … for the expediency of the Army & the Government.'"

Simply put, my father's fears were no longer about war or enemies, but about the power of a single individual—a "same-team" guy—to harm the lives of others. "How they can 'spike' an MD with some Medical Society, some hospital, some training institution, some specialty board, etc. Gosh!, we are all at a stage that to even think of 'CO-gestapo-banishment' (cloaked in 'expediency') keeping us from our Loved Ones, just seals our lips so tight you could get us to say 'boo' to a C.O.'s likeness/poodle if he voided on our pants leg."

This was one of the rare times when something he complained about was rectified. The 116th's March 7, 1945, newsletter reported that my father had been promoted to a captain.

IN MID-MARCH, WITH the Germans in retreat and tens of thousands being taken prisoner, the fighting grew lighter. "For the first time in 3½ months," my father wrote, there were "no patient responsibilities"—the medical staff celebrated with beer and blended whiskey. My father partook, though was quick to point out that the alcohol had "done nothing but make me dopey-lazy." He wasn't going on any sort of "binge," he wrote. I can't help but think that after all he'd been through, he deserved a break, even if he felt he had to apologize a bit for it.

Spring came to the western front. Casualties were lighter, though never completely absent; "when I'm home," he wrote, "ask me about one of the most fascinating cases I ever did viz. a bullet in the abdomen—liver—diaphragm—pericardium—thru the heart—into the mediastinum—& lodged in the undersurface of the sternum. He made it!"

He tried, in vain, to save an eight-year-old German boy who'd stepped on a mine that blew nine holes—of course, my father would know the *exact* number—in his intestine, ripped off a foot and sent hundreds of fragments elsewhere. He quoted a section of a letter from Mom to show his anger toward Hitler for starting a war that led to such things: " … have children to allow some blood thirsty criminal to sic his friends on them, torture them, maim them, & finally kill them."

The horror never ended. "Life just isn't real at a time like this—or maybe so dastardly-real that a peaceful American boy from a small town can't even after months comprehend/'grasp' it."

The 116th was now tucked in tents, not buildings. Snow turned to rain, which turned the roads to mud but, gradually, the earth dried. And with it, came a sense of hope. Oh, my father hadn't suddenly found an unrippled sense of peace; he asked Mom to send him C.S. Lewis' *The Problem With Pain*, his second request. He lamented that "my writing & spelling stinks & I feel I'm loosing [sic] my mind—about the only thing that proves to me that I'm not losing my mind & 'slipping' is those *Reader's Digest* word quizzes—I hit 'em all high."

His letters still had a bit of "piss and vinegar" to them; in response to some article Mom had sent him, the nature of which I'm unsure, he wrote: "Sonofabitch! Shit! Shit! Shit! … What in hell are blood-guts-pain-pleasant death as of March 1945 doing/'costing' now if it weren't for helping guys so much in the future?"

He surmised, in print, that war would be easier for him if he was more of a "hard-hearted sonofabitch." But, clearly, he was getting there, his letters having become juxtapositions of the hardness of war and the hope for a return to his family.

The two themes were carved so deeply in him by now that he could pledge his love to Mom and Thump in one line and rage at the Nazis in the next, as he did in his March 15 letter, which ended, "Oh I love you two so deeply. YOU HORRID KRAUT-SHITS—HERE WE COME."

As IF KNOWING exactly what he was going through, his Aunt Katherine—apparently a sister of his mother's who lived in New York—sent a letter. It was salve for his obviously deep wounds.

"May the peace of Easter come to your heart," she wrote, "even tho' you are in the midst of horror."

Soon the 116th would be pushing eastward, toward Berlin and a victory that now seemed all but assured. "We will probably be moving so frequently & so fast with such short stays at each site that even we won't be able to keep up with ourselves," he wrote my mother.

On March 21, ironically the first day of spring, his daily letter began, for the first time with a new dateline: "Somewhere-Germany."

If, in the past six months, France and Belgium had introduced my father to the "horror" of war, Germany would introduce him to hell itself.

PART III
Dachau

This cannot be the twentieth century, I think. I try to remember the redeeming attributes of man. None comes to mind.
DR. MARCUS SMITH
FROM "DACHAU: THE HARROWING OF HELL"

Chapter 7

SIX LOCATIONS IN GERMANY
APRIL 1945

In April 1945, my father and more than a million U.S. military personnel in Europe heard two pieces of thunderous news. On April 12, Radio Luxembourg reported that President Franklin D. Roosevelt had died of an intracerebral hemorrhage while at the Little White House in Warm Springs, Georgia, where my mother had worked as a physical therapist. He was sixty-three.

Eighteen days later, on April 30, German radio reported that Adolf Hitler had committed suicide in his "Fuhrerbunker" after Soviet soldiers had advanced to within 500 meters of his location. He was fifty-six.

"I sorta felt-for-you on Fri 13th, 1945 when I learned of Roosevelt dying," he wrote. "It's hard to describe my feelings but the hugeness of World-Death-Geography-Life all 'swooped' at once in an awesome/

horrible/yet beautiful manner in one massive gulp, at me. He was a fine Churchman—he lived his Churchmanship (Christianity) far more fully than most politicians are permitted/able/capable of living it. Not until 2 days later did I learn he died at Warm Springs, & I then had an odd 'thankful-glow' that he could be where he would probably have chosen to die."

If my father was a world away from where Roosevelt had died in Warm Springs, he was less than 400 miles from where Hitler had died in Berlin. As smoke rose into the air from the cremated bodies of Hitler and his wife of less than two days, Eva Braun, my father's 116th Evacuation Hospital neared its next stop on a journey that, for the first time, looked to have an end.

The place was called Dachau, a pleasant village with thousand-year-old roots, ten miles northwest of Munich. It was home to the first concentration camp established by Hitler, built the year he assumed power, 1933. And it would be home to the last—and certainly most severe—memory my father would bring back from the war.

By now, Germany's war-related atrocities were not news to anyone within earshot of a radio or reach of a newspaper. In fact, my father had heard of them long before he enlisted in February 1944. Germany began what would become World War II with an invasion of Poland in September 1939. As early as August 1941, British Prime Minister Winston Churchill had publicly warned about how Germany's invasion of Russia two months earlier had quickly turned from warfare to cold-blooded murder; more of that country's civilians (12.5 million) ultimately would die in the war than soldiers (10.7 million). "As [Hitler's] armies advance, whole districts are being exterminated," said Churchill. "Scores of thousands, literally scores of thousands of executions in cold blood, are being perpetrated by the German police troops upon the Russian patriots who defend their native soil."

In June 1942, The Associated Press had reported on the massacre of 342 civilians in Lidice, Czechoslovakia. In December 1942, Edward R. Murrow of CBS radio put it as bluntly as possible: "What is happening is this: Millions of human beings, most of them Jews, are being gathered up with ruthless efficiency and murdered. The phrase 'concentration

Author's collection

Dad at St. John's Military Academy, age, 16, Delafield, Wisconsin, 1930.

Author's collection

Dad in his dress uniform, probably 1944, before he shipped out.

Author's collection

Mom and Dad on wedding day, May 26, 1943.

Author's collection

In Warm Springs, Georgia, Mom took this photo of a VIP patient at the Roosevelt Warm Springs Institute for Rehabilitation where she worked: President Franklin Roosevelt himself. She had the privilege of driving his hand-controlled car.

Emily Cohen photo.

Amid seeing death and other horror almost daily, Dad's letters home to his beloved Emily gave him a chance to vent his frustrations—and he didn't hesitate to do so.

U.S. Army

During the Battle of the Bulge, weather was just one of many obstacle for all involved. It was among the coldest European winters in history.

Author's collection

In Dachau, Dad, left, walked the nurse next to him in the photo, down the aisle to be married to the doctor in front of her. It was one of his few happy memories at the camp.

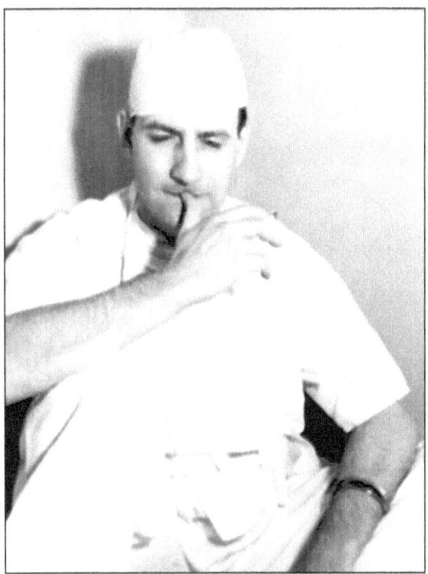

Author's collection

From Dad's pithy letters, it was clear he didn't lack for moments of contemplation.

Dachau Concentratiion Camp Memorial

Virulent diseases were rampant at Dachau. That's my father, far left, in the mask.

Author's collection

After Dachau duty, the 116th Evac got a two-day trip to the Alps. That's my father on the left.

Author's collection

I wish I didn't have to show photos like this, but to understand how Dachau could "change a man"—how horrific the entire scene was—you can't ignore the ugly truth of what the 116th Evac found upon arrival. On the back of the photo my father wrote: "This was seen all over Dachau. The gas chamber is around the end of the building where the GIs are standing."

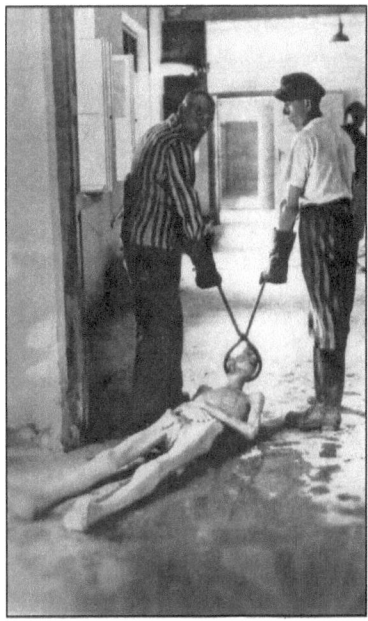

Author's collection   *Author's collection*

This was among the photos that I discovered when I was six. No wonder I could never forget these pictures. On the back of the photo my father offered some context for anyone thinking the men with the hooks—prison survivors—were insensitive. "You, too, would have to use something as speedy & handy as a hook if you had as many bodies to burn in a day as they had to."

Mom, Dad, and Thumper in Bismark, N.D., shortly after my father's return from the war.

In happier days, Dad, Thump, and I hanging out in Spokane, where Dad established a medical practice soon after the war.

Author's collection

This is essentially what I saw when I opened the box of letters that was found in the trunk in the attic.

Author's collection

Balloons were flying at my fourth birthday party.

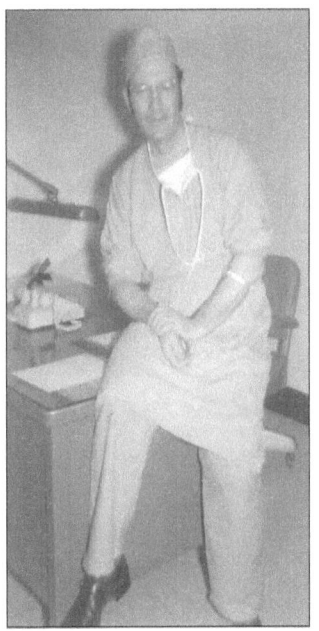

Author's collection

More than anything else, my father loved being a doctor. This is "Doc Wilsey" in his early fifties.

Author's collection

Scouting was a family affair for the Wilseys.

Author's collection

Mom and Dad loved their Siberian Huskies.

Don Bennett photo.

When I visited Dachau in 2018, the "Work Sets You Free" sign made me shake my head in disgust. But it touched me thinking I was walking where my father had once walked.

camps' is obsolete, as out of date as economic sanctions or non-recognition. It is now possible only to speak of extermination camps."

Beyond this network of "organized death," the atrocities abounded: 642 men, women and children massacred in Oradour-sur-Glane, France, four days after D-Day; eighty-four defenseless American prisoners of war mowed down by machine-gun fire in Malmedy, Belgium, on the second day of the Battle of the Bulge; reports by Glen Stadler of United Press wire service of an "open hunt" on Jews in Latvia, Estonia, and Lithuania that had left more than 400,000 dead.

By late 1944, popular U.S. magazines such as *Reader's Digest* and *Time* were publishing detailed accounts of such atrocities, from mass slaughters to U.S. nurses being taken as prisoners of war and having their breasts burned with cigarettes.

"We are in a nightmarish Holocaust," my father wrote on March 23. "The 116th evacuation hospital had moved across France into Germany behind the advancing Allied line. Gosh darlin, a guy just wonders how many times the world is going to ask for the Holocaust messes to be gone through. Each one seems about the 'last straw,' yet more and more come. Two days later…. Holocaust!!!! After HOLOCAUST !!!!! IS JUST WEARING ME TO A NUB."

LATE IN APRIL, word arrived that the 42nd and 45th Infantry Divisions had been chosen to liberate the Dachau Concentration Camp, brittle with mistreatment of human beings. Among other things, it was a center for medical experiments, the prisoners used as "guinea pigs."

At this point in the war, the 116th Evac was supporting both divisions. April had been a hellacious month for the 116th—four moves, none to particularly desirable locations; thus, orders to help units that were liberating a concentration camp could not have elicited whoops and hollers. The hospital had traveled 315 miles and treated 2,070 patients during its twenty-four days of operation in April, according to U.S. Army Medical Corps records.

"Four changes of location were exhausting," wrote Marcus J. Smith in *Dachau: The Harrowing of Hell.*

The 116th's trucks and ambulances had been strafed numerous times by the Germans, "despite the red crosses on their sides and roofs," wrote

Smith. "The long hours on the gutted roads, the large number of casualties, the need for sharing its trucks with other outfits, and the lengthy supply and evacuation routes all contributed to a nerve-wracking month."

But war doesn't care about anyone's comfort. The 116th had bounced from Göllheim to Dieburg to Arnstein to Rattlesdorf to Ottingen.

"We are the only evacuation hospital within 200 miles of this horrible Holocaust," my father wrote. The 116th was headed for "Dachau duty."

On May 1, the 116th was in Ottingen, near the center of the country, when emergency orders arrived. The unit was to pack up and leave immediately to support the 42nd and 45th in Dachau, which was some 300 miles to the south, near Munich.

En route, word filtered back about how, on April 29, the two units had cautiously advanced through the town, wary of snipers amid the eerie quiet, a few white flags of surrender hanging from windows. How, near a line of more than three dozen railroad cars, they had smelled the stench of death. And how, when opening the first car, the men were repulsed by the results of a savagery beyond comprehension.

"In each railroad car were piles of rotting human corpses—a total of 2,310 men, women, and children, to be exact, either totally naked or partially clad in blue-and-white-striped concentration camp uniforms," wrote Flint Whitlock in *The Rock of Anzio: From Sicily to Dachau, a History of the U.S. 45th Infantry Division*.

The 116th Evacuation Hospital arrived three days later, May 2. On May 8, my father wrote his first letter home in a week; he'd been working non-stop and developed a nasty infection on his index finger that made it difficult to hold a pencil. Now, his letter paired the absolute best news possible—"My Most Precious Being, Europe's war is over!"—with the absolute worst: " … we are sweating, stinking, 'existing' in The-Hell-On-Earth-DACHAU!"

He was in the first group of physicians to enter the concentration camp, the only such camp in the American occupation zone in western Germany. At its entrance, an imperial eagle spread its wings wide, as if in welcome, though its talons were clutching a swastika. On the grilled gate read the words *arbeit macht frei*: "Work sets you free." Behind the gate: 31,432 inmates, many at death's door.

Amid his mixed emotions, my numbers-oriented father naturally searched for some sort of mathematical equation to put the scene into perspective for my mother. "Let every word of Jan. or Dec. *Reader's Digest* bore through the middle of your guts—and MULTIPLY it 100 fold. Dearest, the atrocity reports are true—and more! For over eight days I've seen-lived-smelled-'existed' it as one of 28 doctors to try [and] correct the medical-horror-component of The-Hell-on-Earth."

Thirty-two barracks. Eight rooms to a barrack. Triple-tiered shelves— "beds" would be a stretch. One thousand to two thousand prisoners per barrack. What, my father wondered, do the sickly people in these barracks need? Everything. They were malnourished, emaciated, sick. The dead looked more at peace than the living.

On the same day my father wrote that letter, the U.S. Army forced a group of Dachau Nazi elite to tour the crematorium, where its operators had run out of fuel shortly before the liberation—and, thus, could burn no more. That's why there were still bodies in the rail cars. No fuel. And no fuel meant no cremating bodies.

IN THE EARLY 1930s, Dachau, Germany, was a bucolic village in the rolling, wooded hills near Munich. Quiet. Tranquil. Like many places in Germany, Dachau had trees, flower boxes, bicycle shops, churches with steeples, and a river that wound through town. It was blessed with a particularly rare kind of light that drew artists, who found the town of 15,000 people a haven of inspiration. Adolf Hitler changed all that.

In March 1933 a gunpowder factory on the city's northern edge was turned into a prison camp to house Germany's political opponents—a detention center, at least at first. As Hitler's web of influence broadened, however, Dachau became more. In 1937 the factory was transformed into a modern penal colony. Beyond that, an internment camp was built to hold more than 30,000 prisoners. A nearby complex was built as a training center for SS troops; here, guards were taught the brutality that underscored the entire Dachau operation. Offices were added, plus a hospital, shops and factories run by the camp's slave-labor force. Gigantic storerooms bulged with clothes, shoes, and eyeglasses confiscated from the prisoners.

Then came the "punishment barracks," where prisoners would be tortured, and a crematorium, where the dead would be burned. The setup worked efficiently for the Nazis. Although Dachau was never designed to be one of the Nazis' "death factories," more than 30,000 prisoners had died there in the twelve years before my father and the 116th Evac arrived at war's end.

Who were these victims? Jews, homosexuals, criminals, gypsies, clergy of all denominations though predominantly Catholic, and anyone else who opposed the Third Reich. The U.S. Army brass caught wind that the prisoners had included a number of prominent citizens from numerous countries. The intent of the camp was not to kill people; those camps—Auschwitz-Birkenau, Chelmno, and others—were built in Poland beginning in 1942 as a "final solution" to what Hitler saw as the "Jewish problem." But in the mind of a madman, intents and purposes were easily lost in the lust for power and dominance. And so Dachau was no stranger to death.

Inmates—who hailed from more than a dozen countries—died after being overworked or starved to death. Some died at the hands of brutal guards, others of disease. Prisoners were tortured and used for—and died from—horrific medical experiments. They were lined up and killed by firing squads. They were killed in a small gas chamber.

In March 1945, as Allied armies moved swiftly toward Berlin, Nazis frantically tried to evacuate camps such as Dachau, burn records, hide evidence—and kill as many Jews as possible while they still had time. After the U.S. 6th Armored Division liberated the Buchenwald camp about 220 miles north of Dachau on April 11, U.S. commanders began to understand what they would be facing in Dachau itself.

Normally, the challenge of a triumphant army was snipers, prisoners of war, and civilians. This would be different because of the huge number of prisoners—more than 30,000—the Germans had kept in the camp. A special Dachau group was organized for the liberation. A displaced person detachment would be responsible for food, medical, and sanitation matters, a group of which my father and the rest of the 116th Evac were part. A military government unit would organize leadership, and security guards would try to keep order. Looting had the potential to be a massive problem.

In other words, the liberating army did not go into Dachau blind. "The camp is the most important concentration camp in Germany and many famous, important persons and much valuable information may be at the camp," Col. Kenneth E. Worthing, of the XV Corps, wrote prior to the liberation. Among the possibilities: the son of former Soviet President Vladimir Lenin, Jacob, supposedly captured in 1941; Leon Blum, the former French premier; Kurt von Schuhnigg, the former Austrian chancellor; and Hans Gerritsen, a Dutch resister and a close friend of his country's royalty. The camp included people from every European country, plus Turkey, Iraq, Iran, China and even six Americans. About 3,000 of the inmates were Jewish, roughly ten percent of the population.

The report warned that "the camp may also contain, in addition to the political prisoners and Jewish internees, large numbers of convicted criminals. Conditions at the camp will probably be bad, insofar as food, health, and sanitation are concerned."

Worthing wrote that fleeing German soldiers, escaped prisoners, poor sanitation, disease, curiosity-seekers—an array of potential problems would challenge liberating forces. However, when, on the morning of April 29, the 157th Infantry of the 45th Division entered Dachau, what its men found was something for which no amount of "intel" could have prepared them.

That box car with bodies of the dead was only one of dozens. "Most of the GIs just stood there in disbelief," John Lee, a private first-class, said in *The Rock of Anzio*. "We had seen men in battle blown apart, burned to death, and die many different ways, but we were never prepared for this. Several of the dead lay there with their eyes open, a picture I will never get out of my mind. It seems they were looking at us and saying, 'What took you so long?'"

For the Americans, liberating cities in France, Luxembourg, and Belgium had been the stuff of celebration. Civilians, who'd been under Nazi rule for nearly five years, showered the troops with bread, wine, roses, and kisses. In contrast, the liberation at Dachau was the stuff of horror.

"All my men were throwing up like mad," said Peter J. Galary, a medic with I Company. "What a stench."

Ralph Fink, who later arrived with the 29th Infantry, witnessed—and smelled—the same. "The odors inside these cars were unbelievable, with rotting bodies and feces," he said in *The Rock of Anzio*. "Some of our men cursed, some wept, and most of us went into a state of almost total shock."

Many of the victims who were still alive looked like skeletons, too weak to even walk. The dead—thousands upon thousands—would soon be buried in mass graves. Many of the still-living would wind up in whatever makeshift hospital my father and other physicians could cobble together from the remnants of hell.

AFTER MY FATHER'S arrival in Dachau, imagine the whirl of emotion that he briefly reveled in, then felt ravaged by: on one hand, the joy that World War II in the European Theater was over and the anticipation of perhaps soon being home with Emily and Thump. On the other, the anguish of seeing the dead and the challenge of trying to save the barely alive.

And more: the anger aimed at the Nazis responsible for it all, some of whom lay dead—killed by just-released prisoners with shovels, sticks, sometimes only their bare hands. Some of whom would soon be killed by Americans whose anger and lust for revenge frothed out of control. Such acts had to have strained by father's sense of ethics, triggering emotions of justifiable rage against the Germans—and against his fellow Americans seeking to punish those Germans.

"The horror is so unbelievable that they flew in Congressmen to see it the day we came," he wrote. "The famous D.C. woman correspondent ("Life" magazine) ate with us this noon to see it," he wrote, referring to Marguerite Higgins, who arrived with the 42nd Division—and, some would later grouse, was the whole reason the 42nd came at all, to allow Higgins access to a story that would make the Germans look bad and the Americans look good.

"Ambassador (to France) Caffery saw it today," wrote my father. "Eisenhower is expected any minute. All Europe's biggest Cabinet, Ambassadors, news-reelers, etc. have been or are here to MAKE SEE-ING/BELIEVING. Look for me in a news reel. AND!—to think this is only 'The Queen Bee' camp—others are worse though much smaller & it is here the 'policies' were worked out for other lesser camps. In fact, this Dachau is The-'Home' of SS Bestiality—Himmler's 'laboratory' & hang-out.'"

Nearly 100 SS troops were rounded up at Dachau. Some feigned death to avoid being killed or taken prisoner. Some arrogantly refused to keep their hands up when corralled by U.S. troops, muttering to each other in German. At one point, when things grew tense between German prisoners and U.S. soldiers, a command to fire was given and a burst of bullets killed seventeen SS troops. As Dachau was secured, there would be similar situations. My father witnessed at least one.

"In those early 'minutes' I saw captured S.S. tortured against the wall," he wrote on May 8, though he would offer greater detail in a later letter, "and then shot in what you Americans would call 'cold-blood'—but Emily! God forgive me if I say I saw it done in a single disturbed emotion BECAUSE THEY SO 'HAD-IT-COMING,' after what I had just seen, & what every minute more I have been seeing of the SS-Beasts' actions."

In a letter two weeks later, my father apparently touched on the same event—documented in *The Rock of Anzio*—though this time with less affirmation for the one doing the shooting. A soldier who wanted to avenge the death of his brother at the hands of the Germans used a cup of my father's to water-torture three SS soldiers.

"A truly bloodthirsty (I'd never seen it before) combat engineer from California asked to borrow my cup in performing his 'preliminaries' to roaring his .45 automatic right in the face of 3 SSers. Nothing else would have ever 'satisfied' that boy for his brother's death at the hands of the SS."

The Rock of Anzio suggested the soldier was a medic, not a combat engineer, whose brother had been killed at Anzio. Yes, the gun was a .45. And there was no mention of the icy torture that my father felt he'd been complicit in. But such details were less significant than the bigger things at play: Dachau providing my father with all-new grist for the ethical quandaries that he'd encountered since stepping foot in France six months before.

Indeed, my father's stint in Dachau was a crash course not only in inhumanity, but in the less obvious betrayals of rightness. Or were they really betrayals at all? If war muddied the waters of right and wrong, Dachau turned that water into mud. If a soldier used my father's cup to torture a man who he ultimately killed, was my father an accomplice? If a newly freed Jewish prisoner—a man imprisoned, tortured, and starved for no reason other than being a Jew—tried to kill a German guard, was an American GI an accomplice to murder if he could intervene but looked the other way? And if a Dachau citizen had known about the atrocities going on but remained silent, was he or she complicit in the murder of tens of thousands?

In terms of the latter, the U.S. Army seemed to suggest yes. Civilian after civilian—some business owners had benefitted handsomely from providing services to the SS and its out-of-town guests—claimed they knew nothing of the horrors, or knew of them but, fearing retribution from the SS, said they were powerless to resist them. Just to convince any remaining doubters, soldiers from the 45th Infantry Division went door-to-door, yanked people onto the streets, and made them parade by the rail cars, whose doors were open. Others were forced to clean out the box cars.

Handkerchiefs over their noses and mouths, some of the Dachau elite fainted at the site of the corpses. Some cried. Some shook their heads. Most, however, turned away, muttering a single word: *unglaublich*.

Unbelievable, indeed.

From seventy-five years' distance, it is a sad irony that those closest to Dachau could, for more than a decade, seem unaffected by the savageness occurring daily within a stone's throw from their homes—and yet the lives of men like my father, who were there only five weeks, would never be the same.

Chapter 8

DACHAU CONCENTRATION CAMP
MAY 2-15, 1945

Two hundred former inmates a day were dying. It was my father's job to help save as many as he could. They would come through fast, as if on conveyor belts, ages twelve to sixty-five, mainly male. My father's job now would rarely involve the steps he used to save the lives of GIs through anesthesia and surgery; "if you [performed] any kind of operation," he wrote my mother on May 15, "you'd kill 'em." Instead, he would be treating civilians—former prisoners—from myriad countries suffering from malnutrition, disease, and the like. And he, and the others, would need to work fast—just to get the hospital up and running.

As he surveyed the thousands of "walking dead" at Dachau, his anger seethed. The world needs to know what happened here, he told my mother. "You say in your Apr 30th [letter] that newspapers are beginning to uncover German atrocities—why! You readers who haven't been seeers don't just 'register' 100%—I know I didn't. And—then I read how [a government office] suppressed a movie-length news reel of it all. Such chicken-hearted, hindering, ostrich-head-hiding Americans."

The 116th had arrived at the camp May 2, near midnight, the long lines of trucks and ambulances filled with weary doctors, nurses, and other hospital personnel. With the help of the few former inmates strong enough to work, they had a day to clean and scrub the muck out of rooms, sanitize beds, and be ready to function. The hospital was to open the next day.

The makeshift hospital could initially accommodate a few thousand patients but it had to eventually serve 10,000 people per day. Nothing was close to adequate: the necessary medicines, the number of doctors, the sanitary system, the nutrition system, nothing. The medical staff needed living quarters for 20,000 people; the 116th itself would be housed in an SS administration building. A revamped water system was needed. DDT, by the ton, and spraying equipment, to curb the spread of disease, was needed.

As if that weren't difficult enough, Supreme Headquarters issued an edict that the camp not be altered in any meaningful way—for the same reason police don't like crime scenes messed with. And that's exactly what Dachau was: a crime scene, specifically a murder scene. Photographs had to be taken. Witnesses needed to see it. Those responsible for this needed to be tried, sentenced, and, in many cases, put to death.

Turning a concentration camp into a hospital in a day without making major changes seemed impossible. But the 116th went to work. According to Marcus Smith, who was part of a ten-man "Displaced Person" team to enter Dachau with the 45th Infantry, the plan was to initially see only patients with typhus. In *Dachau: The Harrowing of Hell,* he wrote of how once the patients were examined and assessed, litter bearers would transfer them to ambulances, where they would be taken to a particular ward tent for preparation. Clothes would be removed, patients scrubbed, and clean pajamas issued, courtesy of the U.S. Army. From there patients would again be transferred, this time to a permanent ward, where they would have X-rays taken, the expectation that many with typhus would also have tuberculosis. The goal: to treat patients from eleven wards of 1,200 beds each. My father was one of seventy-eight doctors—originally, only twenty-eight, including my father, arrived—meaning about one doctor per 175 patients.

Amid these obstacles, my father did what most doctors had been doing since the war began: Assessed the situation, rolled up his sleeves, and went to work, which, in part, meant giving lots and lots of shots. On May 7, 7,000 vaccine injections were administered—at considerable risk to those giving the shots. In World War I, more than half of all doctors who treated patients with typhus wound up dying of the disease themselves. Though medicine had grown more sophisticated in the intervening decades, the risk was still real.

The doctors' challenge wasn't only helping to keep these patients from dying, it was *convincing* these patients that they—the physicians—could be trusted. For years, German doctors had been using these inmates for an array of horrific medical experiments; these people were, in essence, human guinea pigs who, after such procedures, wound up, at best, physically and mentally scarred and, at worst, dead. Because of my father's command of German, the burden often fell on him to convince these fearful patients that the American doctors were not like the German doctors.

"You have had bad doctors who didn't have your best interest in mind," he would tell them. "We are different. We want you to get better. We want you to live."

The next day, May 8, news broke that the war in Europe was over. If the feeling among Americans was giddiness, it wasn't appropriate to launch a major celebration amid thousands of sick and dying people. And so while soldiers all over Europe shouted for joy and bellied up to the nearest bars, the 116th kept treating the (barely) living evidence of why America's intervention in the war was necessary.

One of the biggest problems was that now that food and water were readily available, patients wanted to scarf it down with gusto—but doing so could kill them. Already, fights had broken out between patients who craved the food that others had. For the patients' own good, the army had to ease them into eating again. Another major problem: diarrhea.

But the hospital wasn't yet set up to do much in the way of laboratory tests to see who needed what.

My father learned that by the time the 116th Evac arrived, the food intake for patients had dwindled from about 1,000 calories a day to 500 or 600. Breakfast had been half a liter of coffee or tea. Lunch, a liter of thin soup. And dinner, one-eighth of a loaf of black bread and a pittance of sausage. That needed to be beefed up, literally and figuratively, though gradually.

SLOWLY, THE STORIES came forth of what life had been like for these people at Dachau. It was not a death factory, per se, where virtually everyone was gassed and cremated. Some died by winter's cold. Some from disease. Some were electrocuted or shot while trying to escape over the fence. If purposeful killing was deemed necessary, the SS most often did it in one of four ways: shooting, hanging, clubbing, or bayoneting.

Not that the killing was confined only to these methods. One patient told of a group of men being sent to a vacant site on a cold winter night, forced to strip, and hosed with water. In the morning, their frozen bodies were retrieved and cremated. Another told of two prisoners who each had taken a tube of toothpaste from a pallet that had just arrived. They were hanged, with a throng of others forced to watch, lest they, too, perpetrate such a "crime."

The doctors learned, too, what the final days were like before the Americans arrived on April 29. The nearer the Americans got, the faster SS troops had fled east. Three days before liberation, 120 barefoot women—the spring snows had yet to cease—had arrived in the camp, having been forced to walk nearly 400 miles from the death camp of Auschwitz. Four times that amount had begun the journey. The others had died along the way or been killed by guards because they couldn't keep up with the group.

The next day, 1,600 gaunt, half-naked "walking skeletons" had arrived from Buchenwald, more than 200 miles away. Two-thirds did not make it. On the same day, the SS forced 6,700 prisoners out of Dachau and into the nearby woods, where machine guns mowed down all but sixty of them.

On Sunday afternoon, April 29, a lone prisoner ran toward Dachau's western gate.

"Americans!" he screamed. "Americans!"

ON MAY 9, 1945, my father wrote his second letter home from Dachau. Reading it, I understood for the first time how he survived the war. Compartmentalization. Detachment. Emotional discipline. Call it what you will, he had either learned—or already had a pre-war knack regarding—how to set aside particular horror so he could steel his concentration on something more honorable. Perhaps it was a combination of both, born of a childhood in which he was basically orphaned and forced to set aside the pain of losing his father and mother to survive on his own. And perhaps it was nurtured by a war in which he was constantly transitioning in and out of the grisly damage done by bullets, mortars, and bombs.

Once again, he was ranting—justifiably, it would seem—about Dachau being the "queen bee horror spot of Europe" and how he and seventy-seven other doctors—medical reinforcements had arrived—were charged with "caring for more than [30,000] derelicts of Humanity reduced to such by the S.S. (Storm Trooper-Nazi) beast." Then, in the next section, he seamlessly segued from the conditions at Dachau to son [Thump] and Mom, and a list of items that she had mailed to him.

"Its piteous sights, filth, disease, horror-torture environment are every word multiplied 100X [what was in] the Jan. (or Dec.) *Readers Digest*. In other words—Hell-on-Earth ... even though the concentration camps are worse. I INSIST you (& all I'd hope) read 30 Apr 45 *Time* magazine & the above *Reader's Digest*. Batches of [Thump's] cute pictures came. 2 packages with, leather laces, candy, popcorn, etc etc. came .... A nasty infection on my right index finger kept me from writing you for 6, 7, 8 or 9 days prior to my V-E letter. I still can't hold a pen decently."

Nobody was more conscious about bacteria than my father. Before he'd left for Europe, he'd mentioned how "they were sweeping the barracks & I'll bet 10,000,000,000 cold-bronchitis-flu germs per every breath are existent." That was a stateside barrack, relatively clean; in some ways, then, Dachau would be in terms of sanitation alone, his worst nightmare. But by then he had at least accepted the fact that "you had to dance with who brung ya," that you couldn't control the war, you just had to try to survive it—and do your job in the meantime.

His life at war was about constant change over which he had no say whatsoever. You arrive in France, tightly bonded with the others in your 116th Evac. *Sorry, we're shipping you to the Third General Hospital.*

You must adjust.

In April, you're not only weary from the daily work routine but from the constant moving eastward, toward Berlin—three times in the last three weeks. *Let's go, people. We're moving to Ottingen.*

You must adjust.

After six months, you have the routine down when it comes to your job, your equipment, your coworkers, and your patients' wounds. *Starting Wednesday you're going to be working in a concentration camp, treating civilians who are starving and diseased; in one day, you need to set up a hospital—but please do so without disturbing any evidence that might help down the line in implicating the Nazis for mistreating these people.*

You must adjust.

You have no control over weather, travel, and letters—when they will leave after you've written them, when they will arrive, and—thanks to censors—what, exactly, you can say.

Now, just as he'd found some sort of emotional groove after news that Germany had surrendered and that their next assignment would be in what my father routinely called "hell on earth," the future suddenly became fuzzy. Talk filtered down from the top that the 116th and 127th Evac Hospitals, instead of returning to the U.S., might instead be shipped to China in the CBI (China-Burma-India) Theater for a possible invasion of Japan.

After more than a week at Dachau, some wondered which was the best deal.

"Maybe God has decided the 116th & 127th Evacs should face this dirty deal for the rest of all warfare," he wrote on May 9. "Many here pray to 'face' the CBI instead. I just do not know which is worse."

As my father wrote this letter, he was, he said, "tasting Hitler's Berchtesgaden wine." And thankful that Mom and Thump were far from this depravity. "To know you & [Thump] are unstarved, unbeaten, un-diseased, un-filthed, untortured makes me thank God sooo."

THE LIBERATING OF the Dachau camp didn't magically make all the prisoners happy. For doctors like my father, the gains were small, like the fighting in Normandy, where GIs measured progress not by cities liberated but by hedgerows broken through. At Dachau, there was too much humanity involved. Too much pain from the past. Too much pride and prejudice. And, frankly, so many physiological challenges—malnutrition and disease—that even those predisposed to seeing the glass as half full were too sick to smile. Some of the now-freed prisoners complained about the food, claimed a particular nationality was being favored over another, or stole from their fellow inmates.

Some wandered the streets of Dachau, frightening the German civilians. At times, people would ask for help from U.S. soldiers to protect them from the freed "wanderers." The GIs' response was almost always the same.

"Your problem, not ours. After all, you brought them here, not us. You let this happen."

One of the goals of the Nazis was to rid prisoners of any sense of their identities—the families they had come from, the countries they represented, the jobs they had done, the achievements they had accomplished. When the camp was liberated, whatever smidgen of self-worth the prisoners still had mustered itself into what could be construed as unappreciative fickleness. You can't expect a man to be starved and beaten and humiliated for years—then suddenly, when freed, flash a smile as if part of the Von Trapp Family Singers. These people had been damaged not only physically, but psychologically.

As inmates emerged from their oppression, it was common for people from *this* country to squabble with people from *that*; having been treated inhumanely for years, they couldn't be expected to emerge without some fits and starts. But such nuances, I'm afraid, escaped my father—at least in regard to a portion of the patients he was treating.

"I could write for hours but will condense it into one paragraph—do you know that after all our work in medical-filth, environmental-filth

& 'psychic'-filth here at Dachau there is a percentage of these patients (it would appall you) who are (1) not the least appreciative (as PROVEN in many ways) & (2) some are so flagrant as to be condemnatory of us (even to the point of threatening to go to their legations). Why, Em, we could just scream!—& even God, I imagine, would say we were justified. If nothing else, we are certainly here in a very full & complete Good-Samaritan capacity, let alone a medical (100% modern & scientific) capacity. Each day, dear, more & more nurses and doctors & enlisted men get burned to the core by this ingratitude & unappreciativeness & unthankfulness."

He was not alone in this sense. Smith, the first doctor at Dachau, referred to a group of unhappy Italian prisoners who'd missed a truck to leave on May 27. "In the past when I had to listen to these complaints I reacted with provincial, self-righteous indignation," he wrote. "We are giving these people the best of medical care and they respond by bellyaching about everything when, instead, they should be expressing their gratitude. But now, after a few weeks in the camp, I am beginning to think that distrust and hostility are part of their sickness—the result of camp life."

To my father's credit, he ultimately discovered something similar, that at least some of the people's bitterness was rooted in their treatment, some for more than a decade, by men whose cruelty was passed on to them like contamination in their drinking water—impossible to avoid.

"It is 'impossible' to see how Germany or a German can ever, or at least [in] 100 yrs, look-anyone-straight-in-the-eye after this Holocaustic bestial crime they have perpetrated against Humanity!" my father wrote. "Why, I hope for 100 years they keep reshowing newsreels of the S.S.-Gestapo-Nazi 'policies' & practices! P.S. And don't be a gullible goat like some who say: 'Why! We didn't know what was going on." THEY DID! And didn't have either the guts to stop it or the passive/non-resistive reveling in Germany's New Glories."

EVEN TWO WEEKS after Dachau was liberated, significant security problems persisted. SS guards, criminals, collaborators—all wore the same "uniform," prison garb—were motivated by a penchant to benefit themselves at the expense of others. Fights were common. SS men who were "found out" might be ganged up on and beaten to death. One was impaled on the front gate. In a May 12 letter, my father wrote of "Gestapo masquerading as a staff doctor in long silk white coat & pants."

Despite strong encouragement for the former prisoners not to leave until they were deemed healthy enough to do so, some escaped. The 45th Division placed guards to prevent that; certainly, the ultimate goal was for all the former inmates to get healthy again and return to their countries. But it was in nobody's best interest, including their own, for them to leave before they were ready. Typhus fever would be spread. Patients would have relapses. It just wasn't smart to prioritize freedom over health.

Such concerns were the opposite of what some Nazis had expressed in years' past. They encouraged the spread of communicable diseases as a means of "population control." Former inmates told of how, until the end of 1942, physicians in the camps were, because of concern about contracting a disease, not permitted to take care of patients in the prison hospitals. Instead, untrained prisoners—often German criminals—were assigned this task. One of the "chief surgeons," it turned out, had been a carpenter by trade. The SS began using its own doctors only when the war escalated and they needed prisoners as laborers.

Now, in mid-May 1945, U.S. doctors preached "patience to their patients"—and to themselves. Word had it that the 10th and 66th Field Hospitals were on their way, as was a mobile unit of the 1st Medical Laboratory and the 59th Evac, to help. Reinforcements couldn't arrive soon enough. My father's unit was used to working with a 450-bed unit; now they were dealing with nearly three times that many patients, the hospital now treating up to 1,515 former prisoners. They were also not used to working with reporters and photographers popping up like groundhogs. Because American brass wanted the world to know what had gone on at Dachau, they were welcomed, even if the doctors could have done without them. At times, the journalists would probe patients with questions that made it seem as if the prisoner was guilty of something and on a witness stand.

At General Eisenhower's insistence, the press was shown it all: the hospitals, the rifle ranges where Russian POWs were executed, the gravel pits where prisoners were forced to kneel and were then shot, their blood conveniently flowing into a drain that emptied into a ditch. It might have helped expose the Nazi atrocities to the world, for which my father was glad, but it didn't help the doctors maintain their quarantine.

The doctors, with non-stop lines of patients, tried their best to maintain the integrity of their operation. Sometimes, though, the only thing that kept them sane were slices of black humor. "Welcome to Dachau," a few of the more irreverent ones would joke, "where you arrive by the gate and leave by the chimney."

The physicians' respect for the patients was genuine, even if at time those patients could seem ungrateful; my father marveled at his unit's commitment to these strangers. The doctors had too many patients coming in and too many not making it out. Though the death rate was gradually falling, scores of people were dying every day. Corpses were piling up.

"At the American commander's request," wrote Smith, "the burgomaster sends townspeople to the camp to handle the corpses .... They fill their cart and walk alongside them through the silent streets and road to a bulldozed excavation. Here inmates dressed in blue-striped uniforms, their emotions hidden by surgical masks, serve as pallbearers. Three chaplains administer the grave side service. Someone throws a handful of flowers over the bodies. The German soil is replaced."

Before my father's five-week stint in Dachau was up, 2,400 bodies would be buried.

"I believe the rumor will materialize that they burn Dachau to the ground!" he wrote on May 15. "It's funny but we all just sorta hopefully wait with fiendish glee for that moment—to see this dastardly place just roaring in flames."

Chapter 9

Dachau Concentration Camp
May 15-26, 1945

Because of its location deep within the country's western borders and because of its ample storage areas, Dachau was home to a trove of items plundered by the Germans from their conquests of surrounding countries: furniture, rugs, rifles, jewels, cameras, binoculars, artwork, tools, you name it. It was also a huge supply depot for SS troops.

If the horror of Dachau was a dreadful price for liberating it, Germany's plunder was looked upon by most U.S. servicemen as their dividend. Americans who arrived in Dachau wasted no time in a frenzied rush to grab all they could.

In his first few weeks in Dachau, this was an ethical conundrum for my father, whose sense of right and wrong was etched deeply. He wrote that he was "not a 'good' looter" because he was "raised 'different.'" What he meant, I think, was that he believed you weren't supposed to take what didn't belong to you; another's man's wife, for example. He detested the sleeping around that doctors and nurses did. He hated the injustice of other doctors, in essence, stealing time from him because they loafed, and he didn't. And, most of all, he had grown to hate war, which robbed millions of life and liberty.

"Each day I'm sorta-kinda in more of a quandary," he had written two weeks before, after the 116th had hit pay dirt on some loot. "Lots of the guys are getting hordes of Nazi dress swords (impractical), sidearms, & bayonets each day & tote them around till they can send or sell 'em to somebody. I just cannot make up my mind to 'jump-into-the-puddle' of collecting (pillaging-looting) or not. Thus far I haven't pillaged a single thing—though I have a few Kraut medical items that have an anesthesia practicality, GIVEN ME by other guys who did pillage captured hospital trains or warehouses.

"Sooo, maybe I'm just as guilty for accepting them as if I had done it myself—yet maybe not as 'guilty.' However, I can say— American soldiers' 'looting'/'pillaging' is of the 'innocent' boyish-Huckleberry Finn type—not that vicious, murderous, sadistic type done by Nazis over Europe, Russia, Africa."

Dachau's loot pushed him over the ethical edge. He took some items and wrote about wanting to take more—even if his letters give you the feel that he was never quite comfortable with the idea, less because he was looking over his shoulder at God than because he thought he'd lowered the high standards he'd set for himself.

Ultimately, he likely rationalized that the stuff in Dachau was there for the taking; someone was going to wind up with it and he'd be among those folks who'd put to good use whatever he took—as opposed to, say, selling it on the black market. After all, much of it had been stolen by the Nazis from other people and there was, of course, no way to return it to that family in Normandy or business in Paris or farmer in Elsenborn. And, well, it was, as my father said, "phenomenal" stuff.

(Long after the war was over, curators at Holocaust museums expressed support for soldiers having taken such items, because some of those soldiers ultimately donated items to the camp's museum that helped corroborate the camp's story.)

> Dear, I just can't even start to touch upon all that is stored here after years of Nazi looting Europe. Let me describe it as thus: if I turned you loose in the Chicago downtown loop of 5 square miles you would find every item there AND HERE ... I have hundreds of smallish items that are of practical value. You might think some to be junk but by & large it's worthwhile. We regret only that we each don't have one freight car apiece to go to the USA ... I'll only mention a few:— a fine deer rifle, twin sweaters for you & I; silk smock for your house-"hasty" work; beautiful & expensive punching bag; I passed over most of the beautiful Dresden ware; anesthesiology equipment; fine optical lens equipment (I "missed" the best); swords-tools-machinists apparatus; fountain pens; lotions. Yet, darlin', I still (by comparison) am a very "poor" looter (at least in actuality, BUT, hold-your-breath on this—I hope, I hope, I hope, my "leads" for about an $800 F2 (lens) camera materializes. Hundreds of Zeis, 'Robot," Leica, etc.(all $300 to $800) have been "liberated" by the 116th, but as yet I haven't "hit it" quite right. My prospects are very good so keep your breath held really tight!

If he finally gave in to what he saw as small-time looting, he told Mom he wasn't giving into something that had become as prevalent as taking souvenirs from Dachau: infidelity. As spring deepened, as the war ended, as the depravity of Dachau roiled in their stomachs each day, doctors, nurses, and enlisted men of the 116th cast off any apprehensions about sleeping around. Even the so-called "holdouts" threw caution to the wind and jumped into a sleeping bag with someone. It upset my father.

Part of it, he thought, was simply the influence of European morals, which, regarding monogamy, tended to be less restrictive than those of Americans. And part of it was war, escapism, and liquor, though he accepted none of the above as justification for betraying the trust of a wife, husband, or girlfriend or boyfriend back home.

The issue came to a head when an unnamed doctor in the 116th—someone my father considered a friend—confessed to him about having had an affair, presumably with a nurse. For whatever reason, the friend had seen him, as my father referred to himself, as a "father-confessor."

"I'm not an old maid or a Puritan preacher," he told my mother, "but I was so 'shocked'/shaken/appalled that he would do such a thing that I just couldn't sleep till 2 AM. I could rationalize all night as to 'reasons' why he betrayed his wife's trust (liquor, war-nerves, 'escape'—yes it was 'Dachau-Escape'—its psychic horror was as driving a motive for 'escape' on hundreds of Americans as much as anything), but I still would like to scream at him—'you damn fool; look what you've done; it's an irretrievable Something."

His anger about the subject intensified. "To look around you in this European world daily—you'd almost 'need' someone to reconfirm the existence of marital fidelity's existence in the world. I'll not preach-a-sermon-of Europe/Army details—you know 'em—I just say one more thing so as to relieve myself by having talked to someone about it: all outfits, including the 116th, have become infidelitous it defies my adjectives to express it."

He seemed to have taken some solace in "a few" others who were "on my side of the fence" on the issue, but with his friend now having succumbed—"BANG"—he wondered who was left to believe in. Beyond one particular nurse, he felt alone clinging to such standards.

Dachau, he had come to believe, was bringing out the best in our military men and women—they were saving thousands of lives—and the worst. "Sooooo," he wrote, "if Dachau can do to other fine people's 'Beings'/Minds/Lives such big things—I feel I can ask you to understandingly forgive me—NO!—not me—my Dachau-'status'—for not mentioning in my May 26th letter that it was May 26th."

It was my parents' two-year wedding anniversary. And even if he had sent Mom a little something a week before, my father had overlooked it on the day he wrote the letter. "Forgive me, huh?" he wrote. For a man who'd been so skilled at compartmentalizing the good from the bad, who could write about the horrors of Dachau in one sentence and his love for Mom and Thump the next, this seemed like a first-chink-in-the-armor moment. His letters remained decidedly bitter, the "Dats me, Bub" humor of his early correspondences nowhere to be found. No more "Yowzzas!"

In an odd sort of way, I believe my father was suggesting that Dachau *does* change a man—in significant and insignificant ways. It certainly would prove to change my father. But the experience's influence on him would come neither in a "what-the-hell" casting off of once-coveted standards nor, really, in a relatively trivial forgetting of an anniversary amid the 100-patients-a-day madness. But it would come.

A surgeon's worst nightmare is leaving something inside a patient—a sponge, scalpel, or scissors perhaps—and sewing the person up. When the patient comes out of surgery, he's simply glad it's over, glad he can go home, and often feeling great. But with time as a catalyst, the foreign object begins its insidious attack on the person, manifested by such reactions as infection, pain, or swelling. And the patient's pain becomes pain for those around him. Sometimes the pain emerges immediately. But often it comes years, even decades, later—and the patient might never make the cause-and-effect connection.

That's how Dachau proved to be for my father.

Chapter 10

DACHAU CONCENTRATION CAMP
MAY 26-JUNE 8, 1945

The more pious side of my father suggested that God brought trials to build character in us, to hone us, refine us. "I am CONVINCED that God marks our lives plenty 'rough' or nasty at times so that we 'wind-up' better—'the bigger end of the horn.' (P.S. I sure 'n Hell can't figure why He slipped Thump a patent ductus, but He sure must have a reason so I will 'blindly' accept His reason)."

The more practical side of him suggested that the higher-ups in the 116th Evac had never allowed God—or anyone for that matter—to hone whatever limited character they had. Leadership, he'd come to believe, was given to the wrong people. "I'm going to tell the TRUTH—the truth about the 'higher-ups' of this organization," he wrote. "My only regret is that some of the ramifications might cause you to worry, but please don't. I just cannot sit here w/o 'blowing my top' to someone."

My father had become much more adaptable to "necessary evils" that were part of war—weather, wounds, mud, travel, damp hotels, and the like—than to man-made inadequacies. At some level, it seems he had even come to terms with Dachau itself; at least on that subject he could flail away at Naziism as if it were simply this roiling black cloud of evil. But his superiors caused him endless angst, because when the odds were already stacked high enough against the 116th—Dachau a seemingly insurmountable wall—his commanding officers seemed only to mortar that wall higher and higher.

"A sweeping summary, first, would be that these 'higher-ups' are some of the most mentally (innate cerebral chromosomes), medically, psychologically, 'Christianly,' socially, philosophically inadequate people that could be put into any one organization!" he wrote. "The paradox of it all is that these 'Inadequates' have surrounded themselves with really good people who take-eat-'swallow'-live in SHIT because of the higher-ups' policies & demands; & these same good-people are just so Christian they realize that a spite-end-point would affect the patients & not the "Inadequates"—THUS they slog through 'shit' for the patients while carrying a burning vengeance for the 'Inadequates.'"

I believe my father was saying two things here, one explicitly and one implicitly. He was up front about the fact that he felt his team did exceptional work, that his commanding officers demanded too much of the doctors, and that the higher-ups did too little to support them as doctors. Reading between the lines, I believe he was suggesting *I'm done. Spent. Empty*. He had nothing left to give, but kept showing up, day after day, to give anyway. It was almost as if venting his frustrations in letters to Mom gave him the strength to go on; what, I wonder, would he have been like without such an outlet?

> Emily, time after time; week after week; month after month these good-people have been asked/called-upon to do 'The Impossible & have done it! But month after month it gets awfully disheartening/unfair/'boring.' For over 6 months it was in a surgical-aspect but for American boys of proven ideals, learnings, background & trustworthiness—for weeks we've had bridges-burned-behind-us

in regard [to the] medical aspect of those sick in Dachau's [30,000+] victims of SS Nazi Concentration.

Emily, this place from a doctor's standpoint is a seething, rotten, repulsive dastardly den of diseases. The place figuratively bulges-seethes-oozes with typhus & tuberculosis—let alone all the rotten sores, filthy habits of these … [remnants] of humanity. Last &, yes, even least, it is psychologically all so depressing & dastardly (as you can guess & see in Amer. News). The cares, cautions, concerns of the "higher-ups" for we personnel is shamefully nonchalant.

Em, we are normally a 450 patient outfit—we already have 1,260 patients & that sonofabitchin' C.O. has told Army authorities: "'Why no! my personnel isn't tired; they don't need a rest period (authorizable & due); they are just hitting-their-stride." Oh Em! That insane, crazy, rotten, "Spartan-life" fool!—that Shit (capital 's'). He is so abnormal that no less than 96% of the outfit (being medically versed) have tried to analyze him not only psychodynamically but even on common human basis. The closest answer is this: he was one of the guilty, "caught," lazy officers of Pearl Harbor. You recall the condemnation that fell on the heads of those Honolulu Regular Army officers for too much luxury, ease, pleasure, comfort, unpreparedness, & lack of work. Well, he must have made a vow that never again would his Command even have the slightest chance of being observed to "have-it-easy," have it comfortable, or have it average (according to Army standards.) … If he was only an admirable-respect commanding type of person it wouldn't "hurt" so damn much; but instead the only solace, comfort, "reward" we 96% have is the patients' gratitude WHICH OF COURSE IS THE END POINT IN GOD'S EYES.

MOST UNITS, WITH the announcement of the war being over, got a breather. The 116th, however, got Dachau, among the toughest assignments any medical unit in any theater would get during World War II.

Even if my father could be critical of some of the surgeons as individuals, mainly involving their egos, he took tremendous pride in the 116th as a unit.

"V-E meant some rest, some relief, some 'breath' for millions—[but] for the 116th it has been no let up & even a psychological 'straw-on-the-camel's-back'—though the camel hasn't 'broken' as yet."

Then he explained to her why he was going into such minute detail about this—because it was the lesser of two evils. If he told her the deeper truth about war, and individuals she knew who were fighting it, she would be devastated.

"Maybe it's this—I write you that (for example) Charlie Gillespie has died of typhus (now don't worry, but in the last War—note last-War—60% of all doctors & nurses treating/caring for typhus died themselves); or that Chet Derbin will spend his life, probably, in a TB san; or Lt. Janie Wilt (a truly fine Christian girl) has had a 'nervous-breakdown'; etc; etc; etc."

As his days at Dachau deepened, clearly my father was at his breaking point. But only part of that was because of death, disease, and non-ending cases of diarrhea among his "walking-skeleton" patients; only part of it was the ugly remnants of Nazi greed, the stomach-churning stories of how they'd stooped to using the skin of murdered Jews to make purses and lampshades—right there in Dachau. The other part was the unseen wounds he was overcoming each time he strapped on a surgical mask. Weariness. Hopelessness.

What further confirmed to me that my father had reached a breaking point were two subtleties involving my mother. First, that he forgot to mention their anniversary, though he was writing a letter on that very day. Second, that—intentional or not—he mocked her at the end of his C.O. rant.

Mother, with the best of intentions, had suggested in her May 4, 1945, letter that with the Germans no longer fighting the 7th Army, which the 116th was supporting, perhaps my father would get a break. His response sounded unnecessarily mean.

"Your May 4th's:—Did I laugh! 'n laugh 'n laugh!—yes, my dearest, I laughed right 'in-your-face' (letter's face) when I read your May 4th's 3rd sentence:—(QUOTE) 'If it's true (Germans not fighting the 7th Army anymore) perhaps your work has eased up,' … Nope! we didn't get into Czechoslovakia or Austria—we 'dropped-off-the-band-wagon' at that station-stop called Dastardly Dachau."

His anger at his commanding officer and the man's underlings had become so intense and so persistent that Emily worried he might do something rash to make a bad situation worse.

"You and I & 279 people"—apparently the '96%' of the people in the 116th Evac—"know what would happen to a certain C.O. (AND HIS DETACHMENT COMDR) if they ever got near a combat front line." (He was, it would seem, referring to what had become known as "fragging," disgruntled military men looking for ways to injure or kill particularly detested officers in battle, where those who carry out the deed might go undetected and others would believe he "died in the war.")

"You have no idea how I have leaned backward (as you belatedly ask) re: trouble of any kind. OK? Feel better? OK! (I ain't gonna be 'banished' [to] a garrison of occupation on Guam)."

It didn't help his disposition when he heard the 116th's nurses, apparently because they had the 7th Army Headquarters Chief of Nurses pitching for them, were flying to the Riviera and Paris for a week.

He ached for Emily, Thump, and home. He did what he could to encourage my mother; "what you have done for [Thump] is beyond any verbal or written expression … .I love you both so violently," he wrote. In reference to whether he might be sent to China, he wrote, "I just ache & scream & ache dozens of times a day over it."

He worried that the 116th's proficiency might increase its chances of being sent to the Pacific Theater. Never mind the weariness from treating 14,000 patients in more than six months, "we are the 'can-take-it' kind of outfit they need in the Pacific."

His advice to her must have been difficult for him to write. "Precious, please, please, please, please 'brace' yourself for (1) saying good-bye to a Pacific bound lug & (2) a fairly remote possibility of last minute rushing through the Suez."

On May 19 mail censorship ended; for my father, it couldn't come soon enough, even if, according to Mom, there'd been only a few redactions. The idea alone of censorship bothered him. On May 20, instead of using his helmet to give himself a mini-bath, he took his "first decent temperature-controlled shower" in six months, which, he bragged, came in S.S. Gestapo Heinrich Himmler's apartment. "Tsk! Tsk!" he wrote. "Something else I need very very badly for months—an Episcopal service from beginning to end in the regular good ol' manner! Geeeee, I just ache!"

On May 22, the Czechoslovakian prisoners left Dachau to return to their homeland, having been deemed well enough to travel. Between May 9 and June 9, some 9,435 patients would be admitted to all of the Dachau hospitals. Of these, 17.1 percent died—nearly one in five.

At times, it was my father's job to decide who would live and who would die. It was part of the job, though he never wrote about it. With so many patients and so few doctors, triage was necessary. I'm not sure my father ever rectified that responsibility.

Because of my father's fluency in German, he understood stories about life—and death—that other doctors at Dachau could not. Though Dachau was a cacophony of dozens of languages, my father's German helped him connect with the former prisoners. Among them: Hans Gerritsen, a Dutch "friend of royalty," member of the 1939 Dutch team that played in hockey's world championships, and Nazi resister. He and my father became close friends.

Hearing the stories, of course, was a double-edged sword, particularly if it was Dachau-based. Gerritsen told of how Catholic priests were put in cages with Dobermans and forced to bark like a dog whenever someone walked by. (Gerritsen's word could be trusted; soon after the liberation Allied leaders made him chief of police at Dachau.)

Gerritsen, who had been a prisoner for four years, told of how an escapee was tied naked to a post where three such dogs, starved for days, were let loose on him. He and the others were forced to watch.

"Hans 'stood' the calves torn off; 'stood' the thighs torn off; 'stood' the guts (yes, guts!) torn out; but he turned his head & vomited when the Doberman had torn the lungs & heart out. The first thing the liberated internees did was to shoot the Dobermans & their horrid handler."

At the end of May, the 116th finally was given a break; the unit was given a trip to the Alps. In a nineteen-hour period, my father saw mountains at Achensee that reminded him of Wyoming's Grand Tetons. At Ober Mening he ran into a buddy, Doby Fields, who joined him for a short deer-hunting expedition; my father shot two deer with three shots. ("17 people"—not "a dozen" or "a bunch"; that would be too general for the man—"could eat venison-steak sandwiched at my 'party.'") He got his picture taken in Italy when the truck driver took them over Brenner Pass on the Italian-Austrian border.

Alas, the trip ended badly. That night, the 116th Evac was evicted from wherever it was staying. Wild drinking would normally be the likely suspect; you can imagine the unit's celebration of finally being out of Dachau after five weeks. But my father said the 116th was kicked out "because there was a 'screwed-up' situation (as always) in the Higher-Ups," and the unit "had to return to this Depressing Den of Dachau."

By June 12, some 166 former inmates remained at Dachau. About a third were still hospitalized, the others still not strong enough to travel. Smith, in his book, wrote that patients who were surly in the early goings had changed. "Now they mention their families, their homes, their plans for the future." Among the former prisoners who'd been released was Gerritsen, the Dutch resister, who told my father that he owed his life to him. My father found it interesting that the man he'd gotten closest to in the war was a prisoner who lived in a different country; the two vowed to stay in touch after the war.

For now, it was time for the 116th to leave "Dastardly Dachau." My father wrote nothing about any last looks, any goodbyes, any poignancy—or "good riddance"—that might have marked the farewell. But the next night, he confessed right up front that "I'm a wee bit drunk—but you'd be too," he wrote, if this were "your last night in Dachau!—Just to get away from here is an indescribable relief in itself. This damn dastardly dismal den Dachau is gone as of tomorrow AM @ 8 AM when we go to Bad Mergentheim (near Wurzburg) for a rest-period & then (P.S. 95-plus % of the personnel is drunk right now) to be going, thank God in Heaven, via the U.S.A."

Perhaps it was a premonition of things to come but leaving Dachau didn't restore the collective soul of the 116th Evac. Just as its short trip to the Alps had wound up in apparent let-it-loose behavior that seemingly played a part in the entire unit evicted from a hotel or hostel, so did the permanent departure from Dachau lead to more "venting."

The 116th's doctors and nurses were spent. A handful went on a bender one night involving drugs. "Oh yes—when I'm home please remind me to tell you what at least certain Americans can 'have-in-their-veins'—what 3 nurses & 2 sgts of our outfit did one night ... to disgrace themselves, the Nursing Profession, the 116th Evac, & the Army."

On June 8, 1945, my father wrote of how "an insanely drunk M.A.C. threw a chair through 3 windows & cast blame on about 15 innocent bystanders. We were so furious that no one (including myself) could resume what we were doing."

At Bad Mergentheim, a village that dates back to the tenth century and was once home to a viola player named Beethoven, a group of docs was trying to put Dachau—or, as my father had begun calling it, the "Dachau-orgy"—in perspective.

"It was unanimously agreed that all we had seen/lived/experienced/'stood' before Dachau was secondary to 'standing' Dachau," he wrote my mother. "You know from 7 months of letters what we 'stood'—thus, if Dachau can 'obliterate' it all, think what Dachau must have been."

"It is as if in the spring of 1945 the world lost a certain innocence," wrote Robert Abzug in *Inside the Vicious Heart: Americans and the Liberation of Nazi Concentration Camps.*

Back home, my mother did her best to encourage my father—even as she struggled with loneliness, depression, and the pain of having lost her dear sister. Her world was so different from anything he was experiencing. How do you relate to someone who'd seen what he'd seen, smelled what he'd smelled, heard the stories he'd heard? How, in a world where you're dealing with a baby who has a bad heart, do you relate to someone who is telling you about Dobermans ripping out the heart of a man? Or about such stomach-churning distortions as healthy prisoners being esteemed by the Nazis because, when they were murdered, their skin would make better lampshades?

"Oh, my dear, try to remember there is decency, beauty, kindliness, love & godliness in the world & someday you will be back in it," my mother wrote my father in late May.

He told her that those words had encouraged him "to my core." But in among his final letters from Europe, amid splashes of 'coming-home' giddiness, there was a portending of darkness.

"War & Dachau," he wrote, "change lots of things that you will have to just see for yourself."

Chapter 11

Weinheim, Germany; Paris, France
June-August, 1945

By July, with the 116th having done little in more than a month, my father was convinced that his unit was headed for the CBI. The silver lining in yet another dark cloud of war was this: the transition from the European Theater would likely come with a month-long leave in the states, meaning he, Emily, and Thump would be reunited after nearly a year apart from each other. The motto among many became "Home Alive in '45!"

Other units were routing from Le Havre in France through the Panama Canal, and not coming home. And though the New York scenario wasn't a done deal—"ninety-seven percent," my father estimated in his numbers-oriented optimism—it was enough to stir my father with giddy anticipation. "Prematurely, I say 'whoopie!'" he wrote.

A week later, my father's optimism was struck a cruel blow. Yes, the 116th was going home. But out of the blue, he was notified that he wouldn't be on the ship; instead, he was being transferred to the 137th Evacuation Hospital, which, at least for now, was not headed home.

It was so devastating to my father that, right or wrong, he compared his pain to that of my mother losing her beloved sister, Clarice, for whom I would be named.

"My dearest One, I have been transferred to the 137th Evac. [on] the 'eve' of when the 116th is preparing to go into a processing & staging area for U.S.A. embarkation," he wrote. "Why God has done this to us is pretty hard to figure out right as of this minute. To make an analogous comparison in our respective lives it seems as of the moment that this 'blow' to me is somewhat like the 'blow' to you regarding Clarice. So many of our dreams, plans, & desires of the last 6+ weeks are postponed/'blasted' into a seemingly unbearable Future.

"I honestly believe this transfer is just simply the dastardliness of War & not any such thing as a 'spite-deal' by the 116th C.O. as he seemed truly sorry, cooperative, & kindly in those very hurried departure hours. It is so hard to rationalize why God wants it this way but we do know [& must accept] that it is His will & best Plan of Life for us."

Early on, my father could find some silver lining in practically everything; his and Mom's being apart, he wrote on October 1, 1944, would "make you & me better people." Not now. Now, he just wanted to be home with her and Thump.

The 137th was a newly formed outfit, many of its doctors and nurses having never experienced combat, and my father said "only a miracle" would route the unit back to the U.S. Otherwise, it was on to Japan.

"Every time that thought-wave of my old outfit going HOME first passes across my mind I have as intense a 'blow' as the first one was when I heard the words only hours after the joyous 116th-news came through. Oh, dearest—I'm in 2 man-sized tents again. The light is almost gone—somehow my almost-gone spirit will come up—because we always will have, my dearest One—All Our Love."

The commanding officer my father had struggled with ultimately paid him a huge measure of respect. The CO recommended him to receive the Bronze Star Medal for what he described as "meritorious service in direct support of combat operations from 30 November to 1 May 1945 ... ." He found the award meaningful because it offered him something he'd had so little of since joining the military: affirmation.

Wrote the commanding officer: "Under the supervision of Captain Wilsey and his associate[s], approximately five thousand procedures were performed by the Anesthesia Section. Due to his efforts, no time was lost in awaiting anesthesia and seven operating tables functioned simultaneously. His superior professional skill, keen judgment in evaluating the condition of patients and tireless devotion to duty contributed inestimably to the success of each operation and were in keeping with the finest traditions of the Medical Department."

Based on what I know, nobody who'd known my father would have been surprised to learn of the honor. That was my father. Dedicated to a fault. Superior skills. Tirelessly devoted. Decades after the war, when descriptions of some of his procedures were shared with other anesthesiologists, they said he was clearly a cut above his peers. What made him different from the man he would become, after the war, was that in the summer of 1945 he was equally dedicated, and tirelessly devoted, to his family—not the case in time to come.

If the honor meant much to him, it didn't stem the pain he felt about not being able to come home as expected.

"Oh, dearest Ones, I've damn near cried like a baby these past 3½ days!" he wrote. "Oh, Em, I love you so, so so—I just can't write anymore right as of now with my emotions."

Because of my father's transfer to a new unit and being on the move from Germany to France, Mom's mail hadn't caught up with him; he hadn't had a letter in more than two weeks. Beyond his family back home, he was concerned about his new friend, Hans; he half-worried that the former prisoner, with revenge on his mind, had "roared loose on a one-man Nazi extermination raid." He hoped to see him before leaving Europe.

Ultimately, he did. He hitchhiked fourteen hours to Holland to do so. Hans wanted him to meet Prince Bernard, who was a close friend of

Hans's, but it didn't work out. With Dad's return to Paris, the waiting game continued, his future still cloudy. He saw a little of the newly liberated city, enjoyed his first Coke in six months, and discovered that his second-favorite drink, next to scotch, was Dutch gin. "Just like olives, you hate the first dozen but then—oh my!"

"Each letter I start in the past days finds my mind a blank—absolute blank—as there is N-O-T-H-I-N-G to write & few things writable are restricted. Anyhoo, I always 'eat-up' the chance to write I love you, I love you, I love you ... gosh! How I ache to get a letter from you—for so many reasons, just one of which is to read something about [Thump]."

When a letter from home finally arrived, he was distraught to find it was only from a married couple in Elko with whom he and Mom were friends. A killer frost was threatening to take their squash and tomatoes. A pregnant friend of theirs was "miserable." But, on the plus side, the fish were biting on a recent trip, the letter-writer reported. "We had lots of good eats, butter beef cream sure tasted good."

They meant well, I'm sure. But I can't help but think that such relative triviality was salt in my father's wounds. *These were problems?* It seemed a small incident, but decades later I came to realize the huge gap of perspective on the world between civilians and vets, a gap that many home-from-war soldiers could never overcome.

On July 31, he wrote his last letter home—or at least the last one that wound up in his trunk. A week later, on August 6, the crew of the Enola Gay—named for the pilot's mother—dropped an atom bomb on Hiroshima, Japan, killing more than 80,000 people. When Japan refused to surrender, a bomb was dropped on Nagasaki, killing more than 40,000. Japan surrendered. Like the one in Europe, the war in the Pacific was over, too, the Japanese's official surrender coming September 2, 1945.

For nine months my father had served in a war zone. The handful of hospitals he'd been with had served, by his own count, more than two dozen units that he summed up by saying "we supported practically every damn division that the 7th Army had."

My father was coming home to his wife and their nearly one-year-old son. And to a future as uncertain as the world's in general. As he'd written only a few months before he sailed for home: "We each, as millions abroad and home, will carry wounds home with us. For you it will be a 'nervousness' (let's call it) ... for me it will be a 'lessened confidence' (decision-ability/decision fearsomeness) .... But I just know we can help each other—cuz we'll need to."

He was right about bringing wounds home from the war. It was the other part—the helping each other stuff—that would go missing in action.

PART IV
Home

Friendship is born at the moment when one person says to another, "What! You too? I thought I was the only one."
C.S. LEWIS
BRITISH WRITER AND THEOLOGIAN

Chapter 12

It was early summer, 1959, and I had just turned twelve. With every stroke I took during my quarter-mile swim across Wandermere Lake north of Spokane, Washington, I thought of my father. How could I not? Even with my ears sporadically under water, I could hear the man yelling from shore during the "pop-quiz" swimming test he demanded I undergo.

"You're not reaching with your hands. Reach!"

"Faster! Faster! Faster!"

"Head down! Don't lift up!"

Nothing was ever good enough for the man. My heart pounded. My arms and legs morphed to rubber. My breathing rasped like someone on her death bed. But to give up was to let him win. And I wasn't about to do that. I wanted to prove to him that I was good enough. Though I wouldn't have admitted it at the time—actually for decades—I wanted to make him proud.

When I reached the shore, I was so tired I slithered to the bank like a salamander, hardly having the strength to get to my feet. I'd given it my all. And I felt good about that. Felt good about *me*. But at the end of every swim, bike ride, homework assignment, whatever, there he was, looming over me as if he was the judge and I was on trial.

I stood, hands on my knees, gasping for every breath. He looked at his stopwatch.

"Very disappointing," he said. "You can do better, Clarice. You *must* do better. I'm giving you a C-plus—and that's being kind."

He shook his head ever so slightly, just enough to rub a bit of salt in my already-painful wound.

"I'll meet you at the car," he said, then walked off.

IN SPOKANE, MY father was among everyone's favorite doctors. At Christmas, our living room was festooned with cards, mainly from patients and nurses, praising him. He was good at what he did; no, he was *excellent*. In 1949, he and two other men founded the Physicians Anesthesia Group in Spokane. He served as a clinical associate with the University of Washington Medical School for eighteen years. He cared deeply for every patient he "put under" prior to a surgery, often praying with his patients first.

"Top of the morning to ya!" he'd say with gusto to anyone he'd meet on his way to his office.

He had a deep sense of justice, a passion to make his community better, and a heart for the underdog; one orderly said he was the only physician who spoke to him in the elevator. He was a member of Physicians for Social Responsibility. He helped create the Spokane Japanese Garden. He was a swimming and diving expert, too. You name it, he was good at it. Bowling. Golf. Skiing. Letters to the editor. Church leadership. Anti-nuclear waste protesting. The proverbial man for all seasons.

He won the prestigious Silver Beaver Award for his dedication to Boy Scout leadership, served as chairman of the medical information exchange for Spokane's sister city program with Nishinomiya, Japan, and was chairman of the country's first medical society to endorse the Amateur Athletic Union's physical fitness program for youths.

He helped spearhead the effort to start a new Episcopal church in Spokane, St. Stephen's, and, in his twilight years, helped design, and paid for, an outdoor chapel outside the church with an incredible view.

Every night after dinner, the man who'd once said of Mom and Thump that "I love you two sooo severely-deeply-violently that I just cannot express it!" would change into his bathrobe and, as a devout Episcopalian, read through one of those Bibles that offers a handful of versions of Scripture. He'd done exactly that the night I was about to fall asleep in my bedroom when I heard a ruckus in the other room. Suddenly, I heard what sounded like a slap.

"Help me, please help me!"

I rushed out of my bedroom. There in front of me was my mother, bent over with her bloody face in her hands.

My father had broken her nose.

IT IS THE great untold story of World War II's aftermath. With few exceptions, nobody wanted to talk about a truth that lurked in the shadows of houses from coast to coast. Many WWII vets who'd seen the horror of war struggled to cope with it when they got home, often taking out their anger on their families. After a decade-long Depression and a four-year involvement in a war that took the lives of 407,300 Americans, the last thing people wanted to do was wallow in yet another conflict, particularly one that could be hidden so well. They wanted to get on with their lives. Get married. Buy a house in the suburbs. Start careers. Open businesses. And take vacations.

Meanwhile, a darker reality was playing out, one that few families addressed: family discord caused by men experiencing what, since the 1970s, we now know as Post-Traumatic Stress Disorder.

"This comfortable assumption that 'the boys' returned home physically and emotionally unscathed, that no one drank too much, or abused his wife or children, could not be further from the truth," wrote Thomas

Childers, author of *Soldier From the War Returning: The Greatest Generation's Troubled Homecoming from World War II*.

The truth suggests that our home-from-war soldiers were far more like the wounded warriors of Vietnam than they were Ward Cleaver or Marcus Welby from 1950-'60s television. Although some men and women returned home without apparent emotional wounds, that wasn't the case for at least 1.3 million who not only suffered from some sort of psychological affliction but sought help through a Veterans Administration hospital because of it.

Though it would be another two decades before the war in Vietnam would lead to the discovery of PTSD, by 1947, more than half the beds in VA hospitals were occupied not by men with *physical* symptoms but with *psychoneurotic* symptoms: nightmares, outbursts of rage, survivor's guilt, and the like, symptoms that were most often expressed not in public but in the privacy of homes. The victims, usually wives and children, were naturally hesitant to tell anyone about such occurrences. Their husbands, after all, were seen as heroic. They'd been through hell. They didn't need public scorn on top of that.

"Just give them some time," the mantra went. "They'll snap out of it."

Many never did. I know. My father was one of them.

Dr. William C. Menninger, chief psychiatric consultant to the surgeon general of the Army, grew to realize that the wives of men who served in WWII were the "forgotten" casualties of the war. "Few gave them much support," he said. "Along with their soldiers, they had to 'sweat it out' in insecurity and uncertainty. They tried to live from day to day, just waiting."

The year 1946 marked the highest divorce rate in the recorded history of the United States, the record not exceeded until 1973, when women's liberation, the Vietnam War, and changing social norms put all-new stress on marital relationships. One study showed that WWII combat vets were four times as likely than non-combat vets and non-vets, period, to be heavy drinkers.

"I was never 'daddy's little girl,'" said the daughter of one vet, "but I certainly was his POW."

I could relate. Though when my father left for war I hadn't been born yet—I would arrive in 1947—it's clear, based on his letters during the war and his behavior after the war, that the Dr. David Wilsey who stepped onto that ship in October 1944, headed for Europe, was not the same man who stepped off another ship in September 1945.

And he knew he wouldn't be. In one letter, he spoke to Thump, saying the little boy was "at the start of a fine manhood & I am on the ass-end of [a] wrecked-fine manhood."

Or, more accurately, there was a side of the man that was strikingly different. He never wavered in his pursuit for perfection as a doctor—and his patients, fellow doctors, and nurses appreciated that immensely. When he broadened his influence to the wider community, he maintained that same noble pursuit, wanting to be what he often referred to as a "solid citizen." At the hospital, in the community, at church—virtually everywhere my father went in Spokane he was respected.

But for whatever reason, at the end of the day, there was nothing left for us—his family. What we got was the wrath of Dachau, the anger that simmered beneath his well-controlled disposition and then, boom, exploded at some innocent offense—if it was even an offense to begin with. *My mother not being able to talk with a friend on the phone? Really?* But he ruled the roost. His regulations didn't have to make sense to anybody but himself. After six months under a WWII commanding officer whom he loathed for his iron-fisted, "faster-faster-faster … more-more-more" zeal, my father became so agitated in his letters home that Mom worried he was going to do something rash to the officer.

She was prophetic. He did do something rash. Once home, and only at home, he *became* that commanding officer. And, in some ways, I became my father—proficient, driven, *Episcopalian*, but ultimately worn down by a sense that nothing I did was ever good enough for him.

Chapter 13

It is not easy writing candidly about a man who, in many ways, I revered. In part, because to do so violates the rules and regulations my father established, and I followed, for decades: he was never to be questioned, doubted, or second-guessed. Despite genuinely believing him to be a good man, I, on the other hand, was perpetually questioned, doubted, and second-guessed—by him. On those three tenets, unfortunately, rested much of our relationship.

And it's not easy telling his back-home story because it might appear to be disingenuous, as if I'm unloading in a very public way regarding a very private relationship, as if I'm taking unfair advantage of a man who's no longer around to defend himself. (He died in 1996.)

When initially working on this book, I had no intention of writing much at all about my post-war father in general and my relationship with him in particular. Based on his 300-plus letters, I intended to write about his war experiences, particularly at Dachau. But as I immersed myself in his letters, as I started connecting the dots of war and Dachau and my father and my mother, a disturbing picture emerged: the man writing these letters was, in many ways, someone I never knew. As I read the letters, that thought kept washing over me again and again, like a riotous ocean wave. The letter-writer from World War II was affectionate, funny, imaginative, forthcoming—all sorts of things I never saw in him as I was growing up.

The operative phrase in the above paragraph is "in many ways." Some parts of the 1944-1945 David Wilsey were an absolute portending of the father I began getting to know when I was born: his obsession with exactness, his thirst for numerically based answers, his search for word definitions, his respect for his patients, his love for God and the Episcopal church, his passion for justice, his regard for ethics, his anger at war, his belief that evil should have light shined on it, and his utter distaste for cheaters, exploiters, and powermongers. (When learning that my mother's best friend was being two-timed, he drove to a phone booth so his identity could be hidden. He then called the woman in the affair and revealed that her lover was married and that his wife was pregnant. The relationship promptly ended.)

But in a few extremely significant ways, the letters seemed as if written by someone I'd never known: his undying affection for my mother, his exuberance at being a husband and father, his humor and creative use of words—little of that made it home from Dachau.

Thus did my "ah-ha moment" arrive: If you're going to write a book that shines a light on the tragedy of war, it's wrong to assume that those who fight those wars—and, like my father, deal with the daily carnage of those wars—can simply leave it behind when they come home. Like an octopus, war's limbs reach far and wide, stun the unsuspecting in myriad ways, and claim their victims not only today and tomorrow, but for decades—sometimes generations—to come.

"War and Dachau change lots of things that you will have to just see for yourself," my father had written on June 12, 1945. He was right, of course. And, as a member of his family, I was among those who got to see it—*had* to see it—for herself. He was no longer the man who, on November 20, 1944, had written, "I may be too exhausted to write on an almost-nightly schedule [but] please know that I'm living & praying every minute for such unbelievably precious ones as you & [Thump]. Whatever God has lined-up for me is just 100% swell with me—all I pray is that he HELPS AND KEEPS you both extra-special-nice until I can come back to Help Him do it."

"Hypocrite" is too strong a word, but my father was blind to an anomaly that I didn't understand until after he died: Even as he all but screamed in his letters for my mother to tell the world what had happened at Dachau, he refused to talk about his experience at the camp to another soul. From time to time, when a Holocaust doubter appeared on television, he would fly into a rage but, even then, he never told us why. I came of age having some vague memory that he'd had something to do with that place during his war experience, but it was a picture so fuzzy that it lacked any kind of meaning for me. It was never to be discussed and he was never to be questioned.

My father's silence on the subject carried into adulthood. A friend of mine had been one of fifty teachers chosen to go to Europe and study the Holocaust. However, when she'd bring up her experience in conversations at our house, my father asked no questions and made no comments about a subject on which he had considerable firsthand knowledge—nor did my mother mention anything about his Holocaust connection. The family had been so conditioned to "not go there" regarding Dachau that I never thought to tell my friend about my father having been there. Likewise, after I'd left home, I lived in Kentucky for three years and had a boyfriend who was serving at Fort Knox, where my father had spent time after the war. But when Dad learned of this, he said nothing to the man, engaged in no "comparing of notes." Never mentioned anything to me about having spent time in the same state where I'd lived.

Though he believed that shining a spotlight on evil was necessary to prevent it from perpetuating, he hid his own deficiencies so well that the only ones who saw them were those closest to him. His reputation in the community, particularly in the medical community, was paramount to him; though he was neither a braggart—few knew he'd even served in World War II—nor a spotlight-seeker, though he never forced Mother to become the quintessential "doctor's wife" nor sought positions simply for prestige, he was more proud of being "Doc Wilsey" than of anything else. It was "who he was." It was the essence of his identity. So much so, in fact, that he chafed when anybody referred to himself as "Dave Wilsey" or even "Mister Wilsey." He was "Doc Wilsey" or "Dr. Wilsey," or "Dr. Dave."

But as he quietly protected his reputation—he saved his drinking for weekends when it wouldn't affect his job as a doctor—he quickly found "whipping posts" to unleash the war rage that simmered just beneath the surface. When, at age six, I found those photographs of the dead people at Dachau and he exploded in anger at me, I experienced the first of many instances where what he experienced in the spring of 1945 returned to haunt him—and, in effect, haunted me.

In that moment, I don't believe he was angry at me. I believe he was angry about the horrors of Dachau, which the photographs triggered. Or perhaps, therapists have told me, angry at himself—for not having been able to save all the emaciated prisoners.

This is the stuff of war. This is the stuff that happens when countries are so blinded by unchecked jingoism that leaders simply look the other way. And, regardless of when or where the war is, this is the stuff that not only follows our soldiers and sailors and pilots and doctors and nurses home, but infects so many others for generations to come.

I can't look the other way. Though my initial fear was that, by telling about his post-war story I would be "throwing my father under the bus," I've come to believe otherwise. The bus metaphor, by definition, implies the "betrayal of a friend or ally for selfish reasons." I'm seventy-two years old. I have no ax to grind with my father, no battle I need to win, no revenge I need to exact. He has been gone for twenty-three years, my mother for ten.

He was flawed. I am flawed. Neither reality, however, justifies my looking the other way. In some ways, Dachau thrived because people looked the other way. Having SS personnel come to Dachau rewarded many in the small town handsomely, so civilians—particularly business owners—were only too happy to ignore the evil the Nazis were inflicting on prisoners.

I can't do that. Even at the risk of tarnishing a reputation that my father took great pride in, the greatest good in this case rests in being honest, something my father's letters suggested he valued highly. I suppose you could say I found myself confronted with my own case of triage and decided it would be wrong to let truth be the patient that died.

Not because to tell it would be therapeutic for me—in many ways, frankly, it would have been easier to let this sleeping dog lie. My story, I suppose, will cause some "friendly-fire" wounds. I agonized over whether to tell just the "hero" side of my father or both sides of the man. However, I know I'm not alone among children of the World War II generation who experienced such familial confusion growing up—the same kind of confusion that has confronted the children of veterans in wars since: Korea, Vietnam, Persian Gulf, Iraq, and Afghanistan. As a university counselor I've seen the scars war can leave on families; numerous college students have sat across from me over the years and described the way war has rattled their family's peace. If my experience can help others come to grips with theirs, if my story can unlock their stories, then it must be told.

"There is no greater agony," writes Maya Angelou, "than bearing an untold story inside you."

So, tell I must.

Chapter 14

My father, after a stint at Fort Knox, was discharged from the service in February 1946. I was born sixteen months later, in 1947. My parents officially named me Clarice Wilsey, the "Clarice" part in honor of Mom's sister. She and my mother had been extremely close, and Mom never recovered from the loss.

My father took a three-year fellowship at the University of Minnesota Medical School in Minneapolis. At age three, my brother became one of the first 100 children to undergo open-heart surgery at the University of Minnesota Medical Center by Mayo Clinic doctors. It was successful.

My father and two of his students started an anesthesiology practice in Spokane, Washington, which lacked physicians with such skills. Spokane, on the edge of the Idaho border in Eastern Washington, would be my parents' home for more than half a century. The birth of my younger sister, in 1950, rounded out the Wilsey family.

My father loved his work as a doctor; I don't say this with any malice, but he seemed happiest with his patients, not with us.

My mother was a stay-at-home Mom who had a knack for fixing anything—except my father. Nobody could do that. Nobody tried. Our family friction, then, wasn't usually overt but subtle—like late-afternoon thunderclouds in the summer: nearly daily rumbles and an occasional flash of lightning and clap of thunder. Though later in my life my mother shared her pain with her priest, she and my father, to my knowledge, never had a day of counseling in their lives. People just didn't do that in the 1950s. My folks were of the pull-yourself-up-by-your-boot-straps generation; if something was broken, you either fixed it on your own or it didn't get fixed.

Our family didn't get fixed. On weekends, I'd often see Dad in the den, alone in his pain, twisted in a blend of anguish and melancholy. He would be bent over in a chair, unshaven, mouth tight, brow furred, rubbing his temple with his fingertips as if lost to some painful memory.

WHEN I WAS six, we moved to a two-level house in Spokane's South Hills. From our living room window, far in the distance, we could see 5,241-foot Mica Peak. The living room featured a giant Webster's unabridged dictionary on a coffee table, in which we children were expected to not only look up words we didn't know but use them in a sentence; my father loved words. In the summer, the neighborhood gathering spot was at a community pool. The only person who knew how to fix the pool's pump was my mother; she just had a "sixth sense" for stuff like that. My mom took pride in being the "pool lady."

In some ways, Mom and Dad were like everybody else's parents: they danced at the Elks Lodge on Friday nights. They took us to Comstock Park for picnics. They took us to church. But our family's "flip side" was decidedly different.

Once, my father learned I'd gone to see a friend instead of spending time with my sister. In a drunken rage, he beat me with the sole of a shoe. Other times, he'd corner me with judo chops flung frighteningly close to my neck; not as some playful gesture but as if he really wanted to hurt me; it scared me to death. But Mom was his main target. As with me, nothing was good enough, fast enough, hot enough, clean enough—you name it. As far as I could tell, he rarely collaborated with her in making decisions. He ruled the roost, and would erupt in anger if, say, he caught her talking to a friend on the phone. I used to wriggle as deeply under the covers as I could to muffle the sound of his yelling and her crying.

That was the predominant emotion in our house: anger, initially from my father, then, as he wore her down, from both of them. Meanwhile, we were to subdue our emotions at all times. "Don't wear your feelings on your sleeves," he would often say. And I mean *often*.

He didn't believe in fun, though he would allow it if it were a by-product of something educational. At Wandermere Lake there was a snack bar, but we were never allowed to buy ice cream, though we were never told why. If Mom bought us more than the basic school clothes, Dad flew off the handle. Even when we did attempt some sort of family outing— bicycling, swimming, skiing—it could never just be for fun. It was always a test or an educational experience. He was always the teacher.

Just as the man set the bar high for himself and those around him during the war, he did the same for himself, and for us, after the war. You could never swim fast enough, pedal your bike fast enough, or eat fast enough.

"You wouldn't be plodding if you were a child in Armenia," he'd say. "They'd give anything to have fine food like this. But, no, you're spoiled." (This apparently wasn't unique to American families. In Ben Wicks' *When the Boys Came Marching Home,* the author quotes a British woman whose home-from-World-War-II father grew angry if his children didn't eat everything.

"My father would slap me at the table for not eating all my food 'when children were starving in Europe,'" the woman said.

To goad me, my father would steal food off my plate. It made me so mad that I would cover it with my hands to ward off his thefts, all of this happening without the least bit of levity. I'd played right into his hands—and hated myself for that. It was a reminder that he'd won.

Once he decided our entire family should learn Russian; he feared the Cold War could escalate into something serious and reasoned that knowing the language could be some sort of advantage. So we learned Russian. Other families went water-skiing, went to the Seattle World's Fair in 1962, had barbecues. We learned Russian.

The two things my mother and father had in common were the Episcopal Church and the outdoors. At the church, my father was always seen as devoutly spiritual. After services at St. Stephen's, he would pray with people who had special needs.

His faith was a part of his daily routine. He would read from "Forward Day by Day," a daily devotional for Episcopalians, in the morning and from the Bible in the evening. But if he showered the community at large with a strong regard for others, we got the leftovers. Oh, he would sometimes call Mom "dearest." He would sign cards AML, meaning "all my love." When I saved a kid from drowning in the neighborhood pool, using CPR based on life-saving techniques I'd learned in Girl Scouts, I knew he was proud of me. He rushed in at the end and picked the kid up and shook him by his feet to clear his lungs. I even made the *Spokane Spokesman-Review*. In other words, at some level, he seemed to love us, but I was continually confused by the on-off switch of that love.

Most of my friends liked him; "buy ya a Coke?" he'd say when they arrived at the house. Years later, a friend of mine said he was the friendliest dad she knew. When I got lost while skiing, he seemed genuinely glad when I was found—though also angry I'd gone off on my own. When I was in danger of flunking a human physiology mid-term at college, he spent much of our Thanksgiving break tutoring me—and it helped. I didn't flunk. My "C" did not thrill him because he thought I should get an "A" in every class. But he helped me survive a difficult class.

But the shooting-star moments would never last. That's what made it so hard; my father was like a bait-and-switch artist, one minute acting as if he cared about us and the next breaking my mother's nose, beating me, or scaring me with his lightning-fast judo chops. I was forever confused, never quite able to relax lest the other shoe drop and I'd get hurt all the worse.

He'd get in dark moods. Every now and then he'd scream and yell, but his default format was brooding. He could sulk for what seemed like weeks. I can hardly remember him laughing. At the dinner table, I'd sometimes try to play the clown and lighten things up. It seldom worked.

If his sense of humor didn't make it home from the war, neither did his willingness to apologize for shortcomings. In a September 23 letter before he'd left for Europe, he told mom how "very sorry" he was for having been a "Chivalrous horse's ass" regarding a spat they'd had. That wasn't uncommon at all in letters to follow, for him to take responsibility for ways he thought he'd failed her. But upon his return his lack of remorse was as incessant as his abundance of anger.

Mom took the brunt of his wrath and rarely, if ever, stood her ground. Based on their letters when he was away at war, the two seemed like equals back then. He encouraged her. He wrote of her in glowing terms. He said "I am so God-thankful I married you!" When he was home on leave before shipping out for Europe, he even changed a diaper, and laughed about it. But all this disappeared after his return.

He may have left as an equal but he returned as superior. And the stronger he expressed his superiority, the more mom shrunk in his presence. Her unspoken motto was: *Peace at all cost.* Mom had one friend, Mary, who wasn't cowed by Dad. Mary would find little ways to defend Mom.

Once, when I was about twelve, Mary warned me to never go to my parents with any problem I might have.

"Whatever it is, he will blame your mom," she said, "and it'll only make things worse for her. She'll pay the price for his anger."

Mom's self-esteem faded over the years. Once she told me, "I should have died instead of [my aunt] Clarice."

"But, Mom, then *I* wouldn't be here," I said.

"That'd be OK."

The remark cut like a knife. But as an adult, I realized it wasn't her speaking, it was her grief. She wasn't herself anymore, she was who my father made her to be. To leave him, she believed, was to disappoint God; she'd made a vow before Him and did not consider it an option to break that vow.

In a word, my father was unhappy—at least at home. I think back to the next-to-last line in a letter his old roommate, Bill Faber, had written to him during the war: "I hope when the war is over you will receive all the happiness to which your long efforts have entitled you." It seems that happiness was available to him—I think my mom and we kids comprised a worthy family—but he somehow turned his back on that possibility of happiness, except when he was being a doctor or Scout leader or some other pursuit beyond us.

When I asked a handful of longtime friends to describe my father in a single word they said: "brilliant," "complex," and "controlling." Another called him "intense" and "compulsively controlling." He could take over a room, not in a life-of-the-party way but in a holding-court way. With hardly speaking a word, he could send the message that people need to understand one thing: *he* was in charge.

True, he liked control. When I was twelve, our house caught on fire. My father screamed at Mom to get the fire extinguisher out of the closet. As we rushed out of the house and stood on the sidewalk, Mom's tears were matched by his angry shouting—aimed at whom I'm not sure. I think he hated it when something was happening that he couldn't do anything about. Maybe that was a carryover from Dachau, maybe he was still angry because he couldn't save them all. The situation was out of his control. Maybe, even if subconsciously, he felt so helpless amid the horror that he vowed when he returned home he would always be in control—and it frustrated him when he couldn't be.

It wasn't until the war in Vietnam ended in 1975 that any large-scale studies were done on Post-Traumatic Stress Disorder. Even if therapy had been encouraged for ex-soldiers back in the 1940s and '50s—it wasn't—I doubt my father would have availed himself of it, because that requires a letting go of control, letting someone else have a say in your life. During the war, my father mentioned a handful of times his interest in C.S. Lewis's book, *The Problem of Pain*, but I always sensed he was more interested in it to understand other people's pain, his patients' pain. Now I believe it was meant for his own pain. The sad irony is that the most transparent my father ever got with himself was *during* the war, when he wrote letters to my mother. She became the therapist sitting across from him in the room, the person he could vent to. Once home, her role changed—as defined by him—from confidant, friend, true love to target of his anger.

He demanded precision. School. Dinner. Going places. It all had to be done expediently. If Mom did something without his permission, he would unload on her. I tried to protect her, though it was seldom possible. It was exhausting.

Meanwhile, he never wanted to talk about the war. This contradicted his meticulous journaling about his army experience, his daily letters suggesting that he deemed chronicling his role in the war to be important. And it contradicted an expectation he'd offered in a letter he'd written to Mom on December 18, 1944, before he'd shipped out, when he thanked her for consistently writing him.

"When I come home," he wrote, "I'll be so overflowing with information & tales I won't know where to start." In fact, he never started. If he saw anything on television that suggested the Holocaust had never happened, he'd become enraged.

"Bullshit!" he'd say. "I was there. It *happened*. I saw it."

It was the only time I'd heard him swear. I can remember him angrily turning off the TV. But he wouldn't explain why it bothered him so much—it certainly would have helped us understand him and empathize with him. Nor why, only two years before he died, the movie *Schindler's List* (1994) triggered his anger. He mentioned that he'd been at a Nazi concentration camp. My siblings and I suggested he open the World War II trunk we'd heard about. He shot us a look that said *Never. And don't ask again.*

Once I persisted. "Dad, I want to know more about your life," I said. He walked to the other room and got a copy of *Who's Who in Medicine*, book-marked to a page with a thumbnail sketch of his academic and medical accomplishments. He dropped it in my lap.

"Here," he said, "this is all you need to know about me."

End of discussion. I was stunned at how unwilling he was to talk about anything about his past in general and anything about the war in particular.

It is not easy, of course, grappling with horror from the past. "What do we feel?" asks Abzug in *Inside the Vicious Heart* regarding people in general regarding the concentration-camp atrocities. "In many ways we undergo the struggle familiar to GIs and wage an inner war between feelings and anger and compassion and the need to run away from the guilt, shame, and fear proved by viewing atrocity."

Later in life, Mom and Dad's housekeeper told me that every Hanukkah my father polished a menorah in honor of the Jewish people who had died in the Holocaust. "When I'm gone," he told her, "please see that the tradition continues."

The man had a heart. But, then, Mom would do something wrong and he'd explode. As I grew up, I sometimes assumed the role of protector. In fact, at times I felt like I *was* the mom. That only further muddled the family dynamics, as did our taking in two family members on separate occasions. The first was my grandfather—Mom's Dad—who lived with us for twelve years until I was about thirteen. He was depressed but only mildly divisive. However, before he died, my aunt—Dad's sister, Sevilla—came to live with us from Ohio. For eight years, she made an already-struggling family all the more dysfunctional.

She was a mess. Her husband was a physically abusive alcoholic. She arrived with two black eyes, her teeth knocked out, and broken ribs; she'd had to leave town with police protection. I felt sorry for her, but not for long. That's because she muddied our family waters worse than they already were. Soon, Mr. Rutherford, who ran the local R&R Store, was calling us again to tell us that Sevilla was at the store and, again, buying wine and putting the payment on our family account; her secret was out. Mom was embarrassed. Livid.

When I was fifteen, while I was being driven by Sevilla to the Girl Scout office so I could turn in my application to be a camp counselor, she was so drunk and angry that she pulled the car over and literally tried to strangle me. I fought her and jumped out.

"You better not tell anyone or I'm gonna kill you!" she yelled at me as I ran down the street.

She didn't like me because I wasn't cowed by her like Mom was. At the time, I hated her for bossing everyone around and trying to take over. She made me angry, the way she treated Mom. If Mom's self-esteem was constantly being chiseled away, it only got crushed more with Sevilla around. And Dad did nothing to protect Mom from her.

The older I got, the more my father started treating me like Mom.

He even gave us names.

"You two are a couple of Xanthippian females," he'd say, referring, of course, to the wife of Socrates, whom her husband deemed cursed with an argumentative spirit.

It was purported that Xanthippe became so enraged with Socrates that she took a chamber pot and poured its contents over his head, which inspired the philosopher to write: "After the thunder comes the rain."

Mother and I never conspired to anything such as this. Instead of pulling us together in defense of each other, his wrath indirectly started driving a wedge between Mom and me. I'd come home and Mom would be alone in the bedroom, lying there in the dark in the middle of the day.

"Can I go over to Kathy's?" I once asked.

"Sure, honey."

Fifteen minutes later, I told her I was leaving.

"Where you going?"

"To see Kathy. Remember?"

"Why didn't you ask me first?"

"But—"

"You never asked me! Don't ever pull that trick on me again!"

Her anger twisted into confusion that was only made worse when she added another element: alcohol. Mom was good at a lot of things, like fixing the pool and running her Girl Scout troop; the girls loved her. So did I. But as I neared the end of high school in the 1960s—I graduated in 1965—she was slipping deeper into alcohol. That emboldened her to speak her mind, though with Dad that never ended well. Her digging in only heightened his anger and retaliation; *how dare you!* The pattern soon was fixed: he'd take out his war-rooted anger on her, she'd take her Dad-rooted anger on me.

Only the more perceptive people, like Mom's friend, Mary, noticed. And I wasn't about to offer any clues. Such denial was an integral part of my survival mode. I could never tell anyone. By now, that was as natural for me as breathing—putting on a happy face and not dealing with the growing unease within me. Most people in our sphere of contacts probably assumed we were one big happy family. Dad had become skilled at keeping his spotless reputation as a doctor and community volunteer.

When I was thirteen my father quit drinking altogether although, later, I'd come to understand that he mirrored the behavior of a "dry alcoholic." Yes, he'd quit drinking—and good for him—but hadn't dealt at all with the baggage that led him to do so in the first place.

Because his Episcopal tradition was also a priority, he remained a stalwart of the church, prayed with his patients, and studied Scripture. But if, in his war-time letters to Mom he'd said "may God help you remember to open the Day Book [the] split second any such category of feelings arise," what he read in his post-war daily inspiration and what he lived were two different things.

At Girl Scout camp, a girlfriend lamented at how homesick she was. "Homesick?" I said. "Why?"

It had never occurred to me that home could be a place you'd miss if you were away from it.

ULTIMATELY, MOM WAS hospitalized for severe depression. Life had become so tumultuous for me that I moved out of the house and lived, for three weeks, with three different friends and their families. I used Mom's hospitalization as an excuse, but the real reason was my aunt. She scared me to my core.

My father's reaction to Mom's depression was less about empathy toward Mom than about making her realize that she was to blame for this. She was the weak one. He was the strong one. He'd shun her, then embrace my boyfriend as if he were part of the family. He wouldn't do that to honor me, he'd do that because the young man was talking about attending medical school, which won him big points with my father.

For a long time, I didn't tell people my father was a physician because I didn't want them to assume certain things about us that the father-as-doctor stereotype suggested: that we were rich, snooty, privileged, and perfect. We had a Volkswagen convertible and a Chevrolet. And God knows—literally—we weren't perfect.

One thing my father did right, however, was encourage me to get an education "so if you marry a son-of-a-bitch you'll still be able to support yourself."

I couldn't wait to leave home and go to college. I had been a good student and involved in student government, French Club, newspaper and yearbook staffs, Junior Achievement, the works. As president of the latter, I'd gone to Indiana to represent Spokane at the national convention and, to San Diego for the national sales contest.

Despite the hypocrisy of having a father who, at home, didn't always "do unto others …," I'd managed to cling to my Christian beliefs, foremost among them that Christ would guide my life. At the very least, I owe my faith in part to a father who didn't always walk the talk but made it real enough that I thirsted for God.

In 1965, I left for the University of Washington in Seattle. The life I fashioned for myself in the decades to follow is one that reflects personal and professional success: I earned a degree in sociology and psychology from UW in 1970; as part of Students for Christian Action, I did social work in a rural residential treatment center for children in the Appalachian Mountains of Kentucky. In 1973, I earned a master's degree in counseling from Eastern Kentucky University. And eventually held leadership positions at four colleges. I was associate dean of students at Corning Community College in New York; dean of students at St. Ambrose College in Davenport, Iowa; director of the career center at the University of Portland; and associate director and senior career counselor at the University of Oregon.

In 1992, at University of Portland, I won the Miltner Award as the Administrator of the Year; in 2002, the Esther Matthew Award for leadership, scholarship, and contribution to career development for the state of Oregon; and in 2012, at the UO, the Anne Levitt Award for making "a significant difference in the lives of students."

After my share of childhood trauma, when I retired from the University of Oregon in 2019 I think I had forged an other-oriented life of which I could be proud. So, why, after nearly half a century, did my therapist look me in the eyes one rainy afternoon and say, "Clarice, tell me why you say you still feel like you're a 'C+' person?"

Chapter 15

A fair amount of my making sense of an often-traumatic childhood has to do with my father, but not because he was evil. On the contrary, because he was smart, charismatic, compassionate toward his patients, and bafflingly angry all at once.

"It would be easier," said my therapist, "if he was good or bad, but part of him was really good and part of him not so much." He was a brilliant man whose war experience, in which so much was out of his hands, left him compulsive about control back home. That, I believe, triggered his quiet anger; he seemed compelled to control but families—people—are difficult to control. Families, I believe, are better fueled by love and grace. I believe he had the capacity for both, but they were not standard operating procedure in our family.

Research I've done suggests that what we went through was far more the norm for families involving home-from-World-War-II fathers than many might assume. Since Steven Spielberg's movie *Saving Private Ryan* came out in 1998, the public has been shown a grittier, more graphic, blood-and-guts view of World War II. But where's the corresponding books and films that show the grittier, more graphic side of post-WWII *family life*? It's almost as if in our zeal to honor the "Greatest Generation," we've air-brushed the painful post-war fallout of war that played out in living rooms, kitchens, and bedrooms across America.

"Despite all the attention lavished on the Second World War and the men and women who experienced it, a curious silence lingers over what for many was the last great battle of the war," writes Childers in *Soldier from the War Returning*. "This reassuring, uncomplicated portrait has been repeated so often in public commemorations and memorial addresses that it has become almost an incantation, more liturgical than historical."

I have great respect for my father and mother's generation; they may well, indeed, be our country's greatest generation. They survived the Depression, won a war, and got America's economy booming again after that war. But that war did something to some men and women that changed them, and the families they returned to, forever.

I've read numerous books, talked to others whose World War II fathers experienced combat, pondered my father's letters, prayed with ministers, talked to therapists, and done deep research to try to unlock the "why" of my father's post-war behavior. The results lean more toward theories than cut-and-dry conclusions, but they are as close as I could come to understanding the damaged soul of the post-war man.

To begin with, he saw more carnage than most. With no intent to minimize what others went through—war is hell, period—doctors saw more blood and literal guts than even medics. My father performed more than five thousand procedures in the five-month period from December 1944 through April 1945. He was an anesthetist on a virtual conveyor belt of men whose bodies had been splintered by shrapnel, torn by bullets, and otherwise riddled by battle, things he and the other physicians and medics did not experience back in the states.

As his increasingly dark letters suggested, that alone was enough to push a man to the edge of his wits—even if, as a doctor, he would have been somewhat conditioned to deal with such. But no WWII doctor or nurse was prepared for the severity of injuries, nor the abundance of them. Consider only one incident, the time he tried, unsuccessfully, to save the eight-year-old German boy who'd stepped on a mine; now, multiply that kind of horror dozens of times a day for nearly 200 days. And just when the horror seemed over, just as the war in Europe ended, just as hundreds of thousands of others celebrated, relaxed, and mentally prepared to head home, my father was thrown face-to-face with a blast of hell—Dachau—that scorched him emotionally for the rest of his life. How could he *not* be changed by such horror?

"At this point his symptoms of post-traumatic stress had to be severe and increasingly difficult to manage," said Debra Whiting Alexander, a mental health practitioner and author of *Children Changed by Trauma*, who studied his case. "When trauma shatters our assumptions about life, a sense of hopelessness follows. The dark lens of depression clouds our view; it may be difficult to remember the meaning and purpose our lives once held."

The patients at Dachau were not people who'd been killed or wounded while fighting for their countries, but innocent civilians murdered, maimed, and starved simply because they were deemed inferior by the Nazis. And for more than five weeks, he treated thousands of these people. He saw and smelled the stench of boxcars full of dead inmates. He heard the final words of hundreds as they died. And, at times, because of the severity of their injuries, he was charged with deciding which had the best chance to be saved with medical intervention and which had to be let go.

Given as much, it almost seems disingenuous to fault him for any attitudes and behavior that he exhibited once he stepped off the ship from Europe. What he'd experienced, you could argue, had earned him a lifetime exemption from having to meet the standards of those of us who have no idea what he'd experienced. What right does a country have to send men and women off to war and then expect them to come home and pick up right where they left off?

But, as my therapist suggested, what tangles the story of my father is that he was, in many ways, an exceptionally good man—at certain times, and in certain places. He fought for justice, built bridges of peace to foreign countries, and stood against nuclear proliferation.

The question that's haunted me for decades is why he could overcome all he experienced in World War II to be *that* kind of man and yet, with or without intent, offered so little to the people closest to him. Why did he have enough for his patients but not for us? How did he go from a man who adored my mother to a man who broke her nose?

It is an oversimplification, I've learned, to lay his inconsistent behavior on his experiences in the war; I had to consider a childhood involving an abusive father. And a mother who, though courageous in forging a career in dentistry at a time when women simply didn't do things like that, spiraled into depression, was placed in a mental institution, and ultimately took her own life.

Though exceptions abound, research suggests that those least likely to be hounded by PTSD are those who thrived in their childhood years. Likewise, those who struggle are most likely to be those without foundations and, thus, have fewer resources to draw on in times of stress.

My father was, in essence, an orphan at age twelve, the hurt compounded by his private-school experience suggesting to him that the school power bloc saw him as damaged goods, relegating him to "outside-looking-in" status. His father was abusive to him, but my father had great fondness for his own mother; beyond pioneering dentistry for women in Wisconsin, she was, he said, a loving mother. In years to come he would grieve that she wasn't allowed to have a tombstone on her grave because, at the time, people who took their own lives were deemed to be undeserving of such. With that taboo now cast aside, he vowed that the first part of the first $10,000 he'd make as a doctor would be for a "befitting correction of the marker for a swell doctor—Doctor Lillian May Gale Wilsey."

As proof that people can overcome their pasts, my father not only earned bachelor's and medical school degrees but did so with honors. How many young people who have, in essence, lost both parents by the time they're twelve later graduated from medical school as members of Alpha Omega Alpha, the National Medical Honor Society? You could argue that he not only overcame his past to become an excellent doctor, but that past empowered him to do so.

However, if that "overcoming" gave him an exterior affirmation of success, deep down he likely struggled for any sense of worth. The test scores, the Alpha Omega Alpha-type awards, the admiration of patients and fellow people in the medical field could give him a "showroom" sense of success, but his warehouse may have been achingly empty.

"He was gifted, intelligent, and became a doctor," said Alexander. "Maybe his success was driven by the belief he wasn't good enough. *I'm not going to be my father or mother. I'm going to prove myself worthy.* But, deep down, there was anger—at times reenacting on his family the ugliness he had experienced. When layers of trauma remain unresolved, the experiences imprint and become a private part of the self. It's often true—what you can't put to words, you can't put to rest."

And the war only deepens that anger. In the Northwest, where I live, the worst snowstorms are triggered by cold fronts from the Arctic region to the north and wet fronts from the Pacific Ocean to the west. The storm that became my father was born of a cold-front upbringing and a wet-front war. On its own, each element leaves its mark; together, they can be devastating.

"We know trauma impacts development, especially in early childhood," said Alexander. "I'm guessing war reactivated early childhood trauma as well, and when it did David had a third war to cope with—the one within himself. Because he grew up with little admiration from parents, admiration from others became prominent. And he found that in his medical work.

"The admiration David received from patients had to be crucial to his sense of identity. The ability to heal others and relieve suffering must have affirmed his skills and been empowering. But in family relationships it was a different experience. He couldn't control the war or his childhood, but he could try and control his family. When he wasn't able to save everyone or relieve everyone's suffering, I imagine he didn't forgive himself easily. Any perceived failures on his part likely tapped into a sense of shame and humiliation. He reenacted on his family the very shame and humiliation he suffered. It's no surprise he refused to talk about the horrors he endured, even to his family. The need to avoid reminders of trauma, in words or actions, is a natural defense."

During the war, he vented in letters to Mom. Back home, he weathered the storm by himself. Few could relate to what he had seen, and he joined no vets groups where some such sharing might have taken place. Was he too proud to admit his fears? Was he a victim of a culture so quick to honor soldiers as conquering heroes that it ignored their inner struggles? Was he emotionally wounded but didn't know how to get help—or was he simply wounded but didn't realize he was bleeding?

Some researchers blame that phenomenon for the high rate of PTSD among WWII soldiers—not only had they experienced horror, but they were expected to return from that horror as if nothing had happened. In fact, *everything* had happened. They'd experienced—sometimes for weeks and months on end—humanity at its worst, up close and personal. They'd seen enemies with seemingly no consciences. They'd seen buddies have their guts shredded, lose limbs, be decapitated. They'd heard soldiers cry for their mothers. Seen civilians, including children, bloodied in the crossfire, burned by fire, crushed beneath collapsed buildings. But at least some had been expressly told upon discharge: *don't tell anyone what you went through.*

It was as if my father had a secret world that others were not allowed to enter, and he was not allowed to escape. I find it interesting, and sad, that we do so much to prepare our fighting forces for war but so little to help them heal from it. In *War and the Soul,* clinical psychotherapist Edward Tick writes of soldiers not needing parades and pats on the back as much as a place to unload their pain. A "cleansing," he calls it. A chance to talk about their pain with people who understand.

"Warriors need elaborate rituals cleansing them of pain and stain," he writes. "They need to transfer responsibility for their violent actions to the society in whose name they acted. Whenever the warrior class is denied such ritual cleansing and storytelling, the war stays 'locked in their heads,' as many vets testify."

Among them, writes Tick, is a Vietnam vet who laments the imbalance of money his country put into training him compared to helping him heal after the war experience. "It takes a lot more time, effort, and money to recover from that than it does to turn a man into a beast who can behave like I did," the vet told Tick. "That's why I never had kids. I can't trust myself."

Read books about PTSD and war and you'll see that while not every person who experienced combat suffered from it, many were forever changed

"I went away a twenty-year-old boy and came back four years later a forty-year-old," said Maurice Paper, another concentration camp liberator, in *Gated Grief*.

For my father, I don't believe it was just what he experienced; that alone was a violation of the decency of humankind. But there was more. What he saw wasn't just horrific, it violated his most *deeply held values*, his bedrock Christian belief of human life having intrinsic value, his sense that we are placed on earth to heal, not hurt. How, he wondered, could human beings treat others with such utter contempt?

In this sense, what he suffered was what's become known as "moral injury," similar to PTSD but different in that it's about more than seeing corpses and smelling death, it's about one's most deeply held values being trampled.

Moral injury can plague someone who's forced to do something against their values, say, kill an enemy soldier even though society and religion suggest "thou shall not kill." But it can also plague someone who witnesses behavior that's in violation of their deeply held beliefs. My father witnessed horrors committed that grated against his medical, religious, and personal beliefs. But, to my knowledge, he never had a way to try to reconcile this "wrong" he witnessed, never had a way to heal from this moral injury.

As the supervisor of the veterans' career peer advisor program at the University of Oregon, I learned a lot about soldiers returning from war. I started realizing my father had to have been hit by a one-two punch: PTSD and "moral injury." What's more, his letters portended just that; before he came home, he'd already told my mother that war had changed him. He warned that he and Mom would have to learn to start over. Only I don't think he ever could find the emotional traction to do so. Once -he'd experienced Dachau it was as if he couldn't get beyond it.

He, of course, wanted the world to never forget what had happened there. The sad irony was that, personally, he did just the opposite: never spoke about it—or his own experience related to it. Likewise, when one of his buddies at Dachau, only a few months from heading for home, broke a vow and had an affair, my father was beside himself. "You damn fool," he wrote regarding the man, "look what you've done; it's an irretrievable *Something*." And yet my father, while not cheating on my mother, committed "irretrievable somethings" in the way he treated us, his family.

Such contradictions beg for explanation, about which I can only surmise. To some degree, we are all products of our pasts. Our most profound experiences, for better or worse, revisit us long after they are over, shaping the decisions we make, the behavior we display, the personalities we imbue, the values we hold. Take my father's unwillingness to let us buy ice cream. Perhaps his mind would flash back to Dachau and he'd think about those starving prisoners. Contrasted with such, our wanting ice cream—an innocent desire for those of us who hadn't seen what he had seen—might have seemed a disrespectful indulgence to him. Maybe his reluctance to let us have fun stemmed from months in a war, and weeks at Dachau, where most were experiencing just the opposite: pain, distress, fear. The children in Dachau never got ice cream, so why should we? It almost seemed as if he had predestined us *not* to be happy, as if our happiness might rub salt in his wounds. But, as children, we'd had no opportunity to see, hear, and smell what he had in war; neither, for that matter, had Mom.

"Forcing happiness, feeling guilty for having fun, and denying others fun can be a sign of survivor's guilt," said Alexander. "On top of this, of course, is the fact that David's own childhood was not fun. Quite the opposite. So, for him, swimming at the lake couldn't be about fun, it had to be about doing something well. He pushed and pushed Clarice, because *if she is not perfect, then maybe I'm not either.* Instead of an individual in her own right, Clarice represented an extension of himself—forced to carry the burden of his perfectionism. Survivor's guilt does not allow for one's happiness without a great deal of guilt or shame. People come home from war and say, 'You didn't go through what I went through. You have no idea what I went through.'"

That, of course, was no fault of our own; we *couldn't* go through what he went through. But we paid the price for what he went through—and were never given the chance to try to understand because he refused to talk about it. As a career counselor, I saw my share of students whose lives lacked direction. But I welcomed the chance to "jump in" and see if I could help them find a vision amid their fog of uncertainty—and I often did. But with my father, I had no such opportunity. How do you help those unwilling to be helped?

I saw my once-confident mother become an insecure "whipping post" for my father. His anger ultimately became her anger. And she sometimes turned her anger on me, threatening—unsuccessfully—to taint me with the same bitterness.

"Abusive anger is often the result of core wounds and powerlessness someone feels in the face of pain, grief, unmet needs and unresolved experiences," said Alexander. "David didn't appear to see his wife and children as people separate from himself. They were extensions of the same pain he suffered. He needed to control them just as he needed to control his own emotions. He may have been trying to satisfy the unfinished business within himself through exercising power and control over his family. It was never about them; it was about *him*."

To get angry at work was to lose his reputation, his adoration from others, perhaps his job. But his anger, like subterranean lava, had to go somewhere. Our family became the place where the lava erupted, his pent-up anger for all he'd experienced in war—or lacked in his childhood.

"He probably minimized the violence against his wife," said Alexander. "Like: 'What's a slap compared to what I've seen? Buck up.' He rationalized his own behavior as being completely normal." In some ways, he became a self-fulfilling prophecy of what he had predicted in his letters—that war would inevitably change a man. How often had he written about how war had eroded the integrity of men and women of the 116th?

At the root of all this, I believe, is a flexibility he'd had in the war but could never develop at home. In war, despite not being in control, he seemed able to seamlessly transition from one situation to the next, even if he might grouse about it. In war, the transitions were never his choice; they were simply foisted on him. A truckload of wounded soldiers would suddenly arrive. A command would come to shut down the operation and prepare to move east, closer to the front line. An order would come telling him he was leaving the 116th Evac to help at a general hospital

But he did it. Over and over and over. I think of how, at Christmas, during the Battle of the Bulge, he and the other medical staff segued from the horror of war to decorating a Christmas tree without skipping a beat—and loved it. In fact, that Christmas letter was among his most upbeat of the war—my single favorite he wrote.

He had learned to adapt. As a military man. As a doctor. As a letter-writer to Mom. In one letter, within the span of two sentences, he shifted from "that station-stop called Dastardly Dachau" to "I'm so glad Thumper isn't a scared-clinging-rabbit in regard to strangers."

That kind of segue was not uncommon for him. He could shift from the pain of war to the splendor of home life—or vice versa—without hesitation. But not when he came home. Rather than change his perspective to adapt from work to home, to meet whatever the new need was, he instead changed his entire disposition. He went from Jekyll to Hyde. When he opened the door to our house, it was as if he wasn't the only one who came through it. So did the Dachau demons.

That alone is baffling enough. But what makes it all the more so is that, unlike in war, when he had no control over transitions, we—his family—were *his choice*. He chose Mom. He chose to have children. He chose *us*. And yet he rarely acted as if we were any sort of priority. Yes, he took care of us financially but, emotionally, we were a confused family.

"It comes down to power and control," said Alexander. "Everything in war is out of control. If he can control his family—then maybe he can control his traumatic memories and reactions to them. I would expect trauma to be easily reactivated for David; his emotions were likely always bubbling just below the surface."

His instincts might have been to tell someone about what he'd been through, to face the demons, to be real with himself and others. But that was risky, particularly for a man who'd hidden things his whole life and who lived in a culture that, in the 1950s, expected men to buck the storms with a stiff upper lip.

"I'm guessing feelings remained off limits, causing him to think: *Your emotions threaten to expose my own*,'" said Alexander. "*If you break down,*

I risk doing the same.'"

It brings to mind my father's edict: "Never wear your emotions on your sleeve." In retrospect, that's exactly what he may have needed—to wear his Dachau emotions on his sleeve and to allow us to wear our reactions to his abuse on our sleeves.

Another inconsistency: In his letters, he saved some of his most bitter criticism for his commanding officer. Nothing was enough for the man. He kept asking more and more of his staff, the clincher, of course, being Dachau. And until the war was over and he recommended my father for the Bronze Star medal, the C.O. seldom affirmed his staff's efforts.

Back home, my father became the very man he rued. He was our commanding officer and we were to respond as if he were such. Nothing was enough for him. He kept asking more and more of us. And he rarely affirmed our efforts. We became the people "beneath him" who paid the price for his anger or insecurity or whatever it was that subconsciously caused him to lord his power over us.

It's been said that our greatest strengths become our greatest weaknesses when taken too far; since the day he marched off to college, in the wake of both parents' absences, my father's strength was setting standards for himself that would force him to be not only good, but great. It didn't matter if it was his stock-and-trade—medicine—or firing a pistol, he wanted to be outstanding at everything he did. But he took such thinking too far by imposing unrealistically high expectations on family members. On our bicycle rides, he would set a blistering pace and be chagrined when I couldn't keep up. I'd want to say, "But, Dad, your legs are three times the length of mine and you're stronger," but that would only trigger his anger or criticism.

My research on my father, war-related PTSD and moral injury, poses some intriguing suppositions: What if we weren't the actual target, but just collateral damage, the victims of "friendly fire"? What if his real target was—*himself*? Despite the hundreds, perhaps thousands, of lives he helped save at Dachau and beyond, maybe, as a perfectionist, he remembered most deeply the ones who died on his table. And he could never forgive himself for what he saw as his personal failure. He took great pride in being a healer and so to lose a patient—or, in the case of Dachau, to lose hundreds of patients—was to fail. He hated that, which, experts tell me, could translate to an odd hatred for himself.

At my father's memorial service, a man told me something my dad said that showed a vulnerability that I never saw in him. My father had mentioned to the man his experience at Dachau and how occasionally, in the triage stage, he was the one who made the decision. "No man," my father said, "should have to decide who lives and who dies."

But there it was again—the one time he shares even a tad of his deeper self, it's not to Mom or the family. It's to a friend's son. Meanwhile, near as I can tell, we became the mirror that he hated to look into, because he saw someone he'd apparently never forgiven—for having survived the war, having watched people die on his operating table, or simply having experienced the horror he experienced—probably all three.

"When someone isn't recognized as a separate person, worthy of respect in their own right, and instead are merely seen as an extension of someone else, it's easy to make them a punching bag," said Alexander. "Self-hate, perceived failures, and weaknesses are all projected onto them.

"David's anger appeared to be rooted in childhood, survivor's guilt, self-imposed perfectionism, and in the witnessing of inhumanity. He clearly suffered the consequences of powerful and repeated life-altering experiences. And as a result, so did those closest to him."

In his superb and soul-baring book *Autopsy of War*, Dr. John A. Parrish describes the PTSD that followed him home after he served as a battlefield doctor in Vietnam. He does so with rare vulnerability, witness-stand honesty, and the precision of a surgeon. Much of his regret involves his taking his anger out on his family.

"I was punishing myself for being unable to save lives," he wrote. "Incapable of stopping wars and being a bad person."

Not, of course, that I understood any of this in my growing-up years. But over time I started to put the pieces of the puzzle together—and even if it's still not finished, I'm developing more awareness about what he suffered at "Dastardly Dachau." When I was young, I had no idea what "Xanthippean" even meant, other than knowing it was a really bad thing to be, but as an adult I surmised that when he began calling mother and me that, it was as if, by naming us, he was affirming us as "problem people." He was elevating himself as better and avoiding the responsibility to change how he treated us.

Parrish, the Vietnam doctor, expresses the phenomenon in his book.

"I reacted to inner pain in a way that inflicted pain on others," he writes. "Pain twice suffered. I became distant, selfish and inconsiderate in my personal life and poured all my angst and energy into my professional life ... ."

Reading Parrish's book, I began to better understand my father. "My fear of failure had become my dominant emotion," he wrote. "I responded with an exaggerated feeling of responsibility for my patients, certain that my failure to know everything could lead to serious harm ... there was time and room for nothing else."

A final comparison from Parrish: "I avoided intimacy. I used professional challenges and simple denial to hide an enlarging hole in my soul. Every day, I was less of myself than before."

My father knew hundreds of people, most of whom lauded him as a wonderful doctor, civic leader, and church stalwart. But I don't know that he had many close friends, in particular anyone who might, in the biblical spirit of "iron sharpening iron," compassionately challenge him to broaden his vision or confront his demons. The only person from the war I recall him making any effort to stay connected with was Hans Gerritsen, the Dutch resister he'd met at Dachau, the former prisoner who credited my father for saving his life. Gerritsen, who became a lobbyist for the airline industry, exchanged letters and phone calls with my father for forty-five years—until Hans died in 1990. He was eighty-two, the same age my father was at his death.

RESISTANCE WAS A common theme in war-time Europe; those like Gerritsen who showed resistance to the Nazi cause often wound up in places such as Dachau. My resistance to my father was tepid at best—at least when I was home. At eighteen, after my mother had been hospitalized with deep depression, I met the psychiatrist who was working with her.

"You're not helping her," I said.

"Your family," he said, "needs help."

"No, you're the one making things worse."

Somehow, I'd conveniently put the onus on the psychiatrist and not my father. If my heart wasn't in it, I usually accepted or complied with what Dad wanted or demanded. Seldom did I attempt to prevent something from happening—say, Mother being mistreated by Dad's actions or arguments. When I left for college at eighteen, however, I believe I embraced another type of resistance—as the dictionary says, "the ability not to be affected by something, especially adversely."

For starters, I broke the chain of anger that my father passed to my mother and she tried to pass to me. Despite my upbringing, I refused to become bitter—perhaps to a fault. I began attending workshops regarding dysfunctional families. I read a lot of self-help books regarding the subject. And between this, advice from my therapist, and a Christian faith that teaches forgiveness, I decided I needed to do something: forgive my father. For my sake—and his. I made a list of everything he'd done wrong in how he treated me, or at least the stuff I could still remember. It was a long list. I then prayed that I could forgive him for each specific mistreatment. Finally, I took the paper with my list and burned it in the fireplace to symbolize my having forgiven him.

Was it hard? Yes and no. Yes, because everyone wants to be loved and respected, and I often didn't feel that from my father. No, because by then I'd been out of the house for more than a decade, and I'd learned much regarding the idea of forgiveness. Most notably, I'd realized that to not forgive someone was like taking poison and expecting the other person to die.

That's not to say that my misgivings about my father went up in smoke as my list burned in the fireplace. Every now and then, the memory of my C+ from Wandermere Lake—or his scaring me with his judo chops—would return. Such moments could pierce me like a sword. But, for the most part, I'd left the past in the past.

I've never hated my father, but I've learned I could no longer carry the burdens that he foisted on me. I've learned to take off my mask, be myself, and tell my story—with no intent of revenge, only of revelation. Of helping the many others who've experienced similar post-war fathers—regardless of the time, regardless of the war. I truly believe that sharing truth could help others heal, just as facing that truth has helped me heal. I finally realized I'd done the best I could as a child, given my age, lack of maturity, and limited knowledge of human behavior.

After I left Spokane and set out on my own, I adopted much of what my father stood for—his commitment to education, his passion for justice, his commitment to God, his unwillingness to wear his emotions on his sleeve. But I also forged a future all my own, a future that didn't include the anger that fueled so much of his own father's life. I broke the chains. I resisted, strengthened by a Christian faith infused with grace and wisdom to treat others as we would want to be treated. And, I hope, *not* infused with the hypocrisy that became twisted in my father's faith.

I can only think of two times when I've ever raised my voice to anyone; both involved my father. I've learned that there's strength in facing your emotions, wearing them on your sleeves. I've found a deep faith in God and tried hard to live out that faith without espousing one thing in private and another to people I encounter. I'm pro-fun, whether it's a summer outdoor music concert or celebrating with friends, some of whom I've known for 60 years. I don't hold those around me to impossible standards. And I've made peace with my father.

The irony, of course, is that what finally brought that peace —what finally helped me come to terms with the man, warts and all—was the very thing I blame for robbing his soul in the first place.

Dachau.

PART V
A daughter's dream of peace

How wonderful it is that nobody need wait a single moment before starting to improve the world.

ANNE FRANK,
HOLOCAUST VICTIM WHOSE INSPIRING STORY
WAS TOLD IN "THE DIARY OF ANNE FRANK"

Chapter 16

My father spent six months in a war zone, survived the Battle of the Bulge, and worked for five weeks in a concentration camp teeming with the same kind of disease that had killed thousands in World War I. But in November 1996 he died one day after slipping on ice in front of our Spokane, Washington, house. He was eighty-two.

When it happened, I was at a women's retreat in southwestern Washington. Meanwhile, a huge ice storm had raked Spokane; seven trees had fallen on Mom and Dad's house, though not injuring my parents. Dad had ventured out to rescue their two Siberian huskies, trapped by falling trees, when he slipped and slammed his head on the ice.

When a woman at the retreat came into the room as if looking for someone, I immediately had a premonition that I was that someone. He was in the hospital, my mother told me, and on life support; doctors believed it was only a matter of time until he passed.

Because of the ice storm, it was virtually impossible to fly or drive to Spokane. I decided that the place for me was right there, at the retreat. I laid on my bed, stared at the ceiling, and felt as if this was a good place to be. I didn't want to draw attention to myself nor to distract the other women from their focus on deepening their relationships with God.

I joined the group later for an exercise in which the leader placed a basin in front of us and encouraged us to put something in it that we wanted to release to God, a burden, an object representing someone we needed to forgive. She gave us time to ponder what that might be. Those who chose to participate then walked to the basin, placed their item or items in it, and explained why they had chosen what they had.

Soon it was my turn. I emptied a bottle of pills. A few women in the group squinted their eyes in puzzlement.

"My father," I said, "was a doctor. And a great one. He was committed to being a 'Hippocrateon doctor,' meaning he was deeply committed to the healing and well-being of his patients; they were his priority. But to me he could be a real pill."

It was not easy saying this because the man had instilled in me the idea that we weren't to share our emotions. And yet here I was, sharing this in front of women from my church—and it wasn't a particularly flattering assessment of my father. But it was one step in my healing process.

The last time I'd seen him before the fall he had done something that was remarkable because of its rarity: He'd broken out in a huge belly laugh over something I can't even remember. He rarely did that. I rarely remember my father with a smile on his face.

Now, in a phone call I'd arranged with my mother, I finally mustered the courage to tell him something I needed to say. Mom put the phone to his ear; he couldn't hold it himself.

"Dad," I said, "I want to thank you for the good things you contributed to my life as a father."

No response, nor did I expect one; Mom wasn't even sure he was still conscious. There was, of course, more. I took a deep breath.

"And, Dad, I forgive you for other ways you treated me."

Again, no response. I believe at some level—I *hope* at some level—he heard me. If not, that's all right; either way, it was important for me to say these final words to him. I said goodbye to my mother and gently hung up the phone.

He died three hours later.

I had often wondered how I would react when he passed. My reaction didn't surprise me. I was sad—that he was gone and that we hadn't had a better relationship. I cried. But I was also relieved that I didn't have to worry about him anymore; he'd have been lost if Mom had gone first. In retrospect, that seems strange—that, in the end, he was so dependent on her. Just as he'd been in the beginning, writing the letters home of how he "ached" for her and Thump. It was just all the time in between that he went missing.

IT WOULD BE ten years before I would see him next—in a sense. In 2006, I was at a conference in Baltimore in relation to my position as associate director of the Career Center at the University of Oregon. With an afternoon to sightsee, I decided to visit the Smithsonian Institution in Washington, D.C. But when the Metrorail driver announced an earlier stop as including the U.S. Holocaust Memorial Museum, I instinctively exited the train—a total "impulse" thing—and went to it. I knew that my father had some connection to a concentration camp during World War II, but the specifics were fuzzy at best.

I was waiting in line for the elevator to take museum visitors to the fourth floor, surrounded by a throng of people, when a complete stranger invited me to come to the front. Had that not happened, the next thing would not have happened. Suddenly, there on a TV screen outside the elevator, I saw my father in a newsreel from Dachau. He was walking by two stripe-suited former prisoners who were talking to each other. The image was unmistakably my father, even though, of course, I hadn't even been born at the time.

(Three years later, when I first read his letters, I would be stunned to read this in his first one from Dachau, regarding General Eisenhower and congressmen expected to arrive any moment. "Look for me," he'd written, "in the newsreel." I wanted to say: *Dad, I saw you, I saw you!*)

In D.C., seeing that image filled me with a sense of pride, wonder, *connection*. I watched the footage over and over, perhaps two dozen times, as my heart pounded, my knees weakened, my skin turned clammy. (Later, a museum public-relations person with whom I shared my discovery said to me, "You had such a visceral reaction, I'm sure your spirit knew it was your father.")

"That's my dad," I said to the woman next to me outside the elevator.

"Oh, my gosh," she said. "This means so much to me, connecting with someone whose father was actually *there*."

She wrapped me in a huge hug, her eyes wet with tears. And to think that if that man had not asked me to come to the front of the line, I might not have seen the video screen. It was, I believe, a "God thing," the first of many on a journey that, at the time, I didn't even realize I'd begun.

That moment reawakened in me an interest in my father and his connection to this place where he clearly had been. It also unearthed some memories that time had long since buried, most significantly the day fifty-three years before when, as a six-year-old, I'd discovered the photos of the bodies at Dachau. At the time, it was the angriest I'd ever seen my father. Only now, more than a half-century removed, I better understood why.

Later, in Spokane to see my mother, I remembered the photos I'd seen as a little girl. I told her about seeing Dad in the newsreel in Washington, D.C.

"Interesting," she said.

"Mom," I said, "could I look for that war trunk that Dad saved?"

"No!" she said emphatically. She never said another word about it. Near the end of her life, she steadfastly stuck to my father's edict that we weren't "going there." If someone said something about the Holocaust, she might say, "that's interesting." Nothing more. And yet she knew; she'd read the letters.

On September 11, 2007, I experienced my own personal 9/11: the diagnosis was endometrial cancer. Seeing the footage of my father had energized me to at least seek more information about his experience at Dachau, but news of the cancer quickly put the kibosh to that. I would have five surgeries over the next few years. Between the cancer, surgeries, and work, Dachau was relegated to my mental attic, though I hadn't forgotten it was still there.

In October 2008, a day after we celebrated Mom's ninety-second birthday with her in the hospital—and with my cancer beaten—she died. A harpist was playing and singing the 23rd Psalm as my mom took her last breath. I was sad, of course, but relieved that the orthopedic pain that had forced her into a wheelchair was gone.

Nine months later, as we were cleaning out the house so the new owners could move in, my brother found the trunk and, opened it. I was in another part of the house, the living room. Suddenly, my sister came running down the hallway toward me, obviously flustered.

"Oh, no," she said. "I think I'm going to be sick."

"What is it?" I asked.

She nodded behind her. There was my brother standing on the attic steps, holding a huge Nazi flag bearing a swastika. At the sight of it I felt as if kicked in the gut. My brother and sister had obviously opened the trunk. We knew there'd been this trunk of our father's that contained some World War II artifacts, but the few times it had been mentioned, he'd told us in no uncertain terms that it was never to be opened.

The trunk included an array of memorabilia. It was late in the day. We were tired and way behind in our cleanup. As we finished the last of the cleaning, several of the boxes wound up in my car, seemingly by random selection.

Three months later, on a rainy October day, I decided to open them—boxes that had gone from Europe to Bismarck to Minneapolis and to two houses in Spokane, one of which nearly burned down in a fire. At any move along the way, my father and mother could have tossed them. The fire could have destroyed them. I've long wondered: If Dad wanted to hide the fact that he'd been at Dachau, why didn't he get rid of them? Or, after he died, why hadn't Mom discarded them?

When I opened the first box my eyes widened. It was full of letters my father had written to my mother during the war—more than 300. In the middle of the stack was something else. I reached down and pulled out a few dozen photos. My gut wrenched in horror. They were the photos of the dead concentration-camp prisoners that I had seen when I was six, taken, most likely, by my father. The photos I'd secretly been hoping I might find as we closed up the house.

I began sobbing, something I rarely do. ("Clarice, don't wear your emotions on your sleeves!") When I found the letters, I wondered if they would give me a clue about what it had been like, surviving a war whose ultimate horror—at least for my father—had been this place known as Dachau.

My mother had obviously saved the letters since they were written to her. They were neatly organized in chronological order. Somewhere from my past, I remembered the liberation was late April or early May 1945. I sifted through the stack and pulled out one dated May 8, 1945; it was about coming into Dachau as liberators and seeing the "40,000+ wrecks of humanity," prisoners who'd been turned into "depraved beasts" by the Nazis.

Oh. My. God. This was why my father would erupt into rage whenever he saw something on TV involving Holocaust deniers. This, perhaps, was why my father would erupt into rage, period.

Not only had I seen him in the newsreel footage, but now I had his analysis of what he'd experienced. When I opened that box, it proved to be part Pandora's Box and part Rubik's Cube. As much as the letters showed me a warmer, wiser side of my father that I'd never known, they also forced me to confront a painful past. They challenged me to try and figure out an enigmatic father who I'd always known to be complex, but now, I realized, was even more complex than I'd imagined.

On some level, I sensed a need to be my father's voice, to remind people what had happened—and that such atrocities can happen again. But where to begin? How to find a platform? Who do you speak to and how do you find groups who would want to hear the story?

As I pondered such stories, I was inspired by Leila Levinson's book, *Gated Grief: The Daughter of a GI Concentration Camp Liberator Discovers a Legacy of Trauma*. Levinson, too, discovered her doctor-father's concentration-camp photos, then interviewed other soldiers who'd experienced the liberation of such camps.

In one case, she writes of Rabbi Eli Heimberg, who, as part of the 42nd Division, also was at Dachau when it was liberated. He, too, wrote letters home to his wife that neither looked at once he returned. While in Germany on business, however, he met a businessman who referred to the Holocaust as "Jewish fiction."

"At that moment," he told Levinson, "I decided there was reason for me to talk about what I had seen."

Later, when I was trying to figure out what to do with these letters—perhaps give them to a historical organization or write a book—outside forces intervened, opening up opportunities that otherwise might not have existed. In 2015, a journalist-friend of my brother approached me about his wanting to do a story on my father's letters for *Time* magazine. It was to be in conjunction with the seventieth anniversary of Dachau's liberation.

The article, by Steve Friess, ultimately was published in the *New Republic,* not *Time.* The floodgates had been opened. Other media outlets approached me and my siblings about doing stories of their own. When *The Register-Guard,* the paper in my home of Eugene, did one, I was contacted by Deborah Green, Ph.D., chair of the Judaic Studies program at the University of Oregon, where I taught. She asked me to speak at a Holocaust Remembrance Day event the next spring. In my career as an educator, I'd grown comfortable in front of audiences, and I didn't hesitate to accept the offer. Although at times Dr. David Wilsey might have disappointed me as a father, in the context of Dachau I saw him as a hero.

The whirlwind had begun. Doors were opening up left and right and I felt called to enter. Soon I was speaking to a home school association and a museum in Wisconsin, Skyping to classes at the University of Minnesota, talking to people in New York who'd offered to digitize the letters. An attorney in Eugene approached me about helping me acquire the rights to the letters from my brother and sister, which I did with their blessing. A handful of organizations and museums contacted me about the possible donation of the letters to them so my father's words could be shared with a wider audience. I accepted the offer to join the speakers' bureau for the Holocaust Center for Humanity in Seattle and the Oregon Jewish Museum and the Center for Holocaust Education in Portland.

Amid the rush of speaking engagements, I realized I was experiencing the privilege of being the voice of my father, who had told my mother, "Tell thousands so that millions will know what Dachau is and never forget … ."

Ultimately, I chose to give the letters to the Holocaust Center for Humanity in Seattle because it was located in the state where my father spent the last fifty years of his life. This was a Washington story and the letters deserved to stay there.

Soon I was creating a Power Point for my talks, setting up more speaking sessions at colleges, high schools, synagogues, museums, libraries, churches—basically with anyone wanting to hear the story. One event led to another and soon I had dozens of speaking engagements on my calendar; dozens more would follow. Through it all, I kept feeling a sense that this was what I was supposed to be doing, that God was shining a light on a new pathway for me. I was already contemplating retiring from my job at the University of Oregon; this, I realized, would ease the segue, continuing to give me a strong sense of purpose, and involve the young people I so enjoyed working with. I like their energy. I like their curiosity. When you look for the best in them, they usually give you their best.

Once I spoke in front of about a hundred high schoolers, students three generations removed from World War II. But these students were absolutely locked into my presentation, and when it was over they peppered me with all sorts of great questions. That hasn't always been the case with younger audiences like this; some, I believe, have been too intimidated to ask a question because the subject was so foreign to them. They don't want to look foolish in front of their peers. Even then, audiences had listened intently and respectfully.

After I spoke at Eugene's largest synagogue, Temple Beth Israel, a political science professor at the University of Oregon contacted me.

"My father, too, was a physician at Dachau," said Gerald Berk. "Unfortunately, by the time I had an interest in the subject he had died of Alzheimers. Could I meet you to talk about the camp and your father's experience there?"

I was more than happy to meet with him. I arrived at the restaurant with newspaper articles, sample letters from my father, and two large photos showing groups of doctors who had worked in the camp after liberation. He carefully looked at both pictures, his eyes squinting a tad as he leaned closer to them.

"This," he said, pointing to a man, "is my father."

Our eyes grew misty. His father was right next to mine. What were the chances? The two of us had worked on the same campus together for twenty years; we'd probably passed each other on the walkways, never knowing what we shared in common.

At the church I attend, St. Matthew's Episcopal, people who'd heard about my father's letters began asking me two questions: Was I considering writing a book and was I going to go to Dachau, which had been turned into a memorial and open for tours since 1965? Neither seemed practical; I was too busy and, at the time, a trip to Europe seemed too much of a strain for my budget. Perhaps some other time, I told myself.

When Warren and Connie, a couple I knew from church, returned from a visit to Germany, they brought me Smith's *Dachau: The Harrowing of Hell*. It helped me better understand Dachau and the doctors whose job it was to try to save the thousands of prisoners who'd suddenly been freed by American armies.

I contacted the publisher with hopes of being able to get in touch with an adult child of Smith; I assumed the author himself had passed. After a few months, I'd given up hope but a year after I made the request, a daughter contacted me. By phone and e-mail, we began an interesting exchange about our respective fathers.

When I'd spoken at the event at Temple Beth Israel in Eugene, I'd mentioned the book and told the story of having a chance to connect with the author's daughter, Pat. A cousin of Pat's, it turned out, was in the Temple Beth Israel audience; she'd lost contact with Pat over the years and was thrilled to hear that I had contact information for her. The two, who had played together as children at Dr. Smith's house in California, were able to reconnect.

I so enjoyed getting to know someone whose father, like mine, had been at Dachau; in fact, I made plans to fly to Oakland, California, to see her. But it never happened. She'd told me, almost in passing, that she had cancer, though I didn't get the idea it was terminal. I was wrong. Shortly before I was to leave, I was saddened to hear from her husband that she'd died.

Amid such hurt, however, my "Dachau journey" rejuvenated me. Discovering these commonalities was a win-win; I was making connections with people that enriched my life, and I was enriching the lives of others.

When Warren and Connie talked about their experience in Germany, I began getting increasingly intrigued by the idea of going myself. And when they invited me to go with them, the decision was made. I was going. Never mind that I really couldn't afford it; with airline miles, the round trip cost me only $200.

Like the prisoners, we arrived by train—but a nice train that served snacks, not a cattle car where people were forced to, as my father would say, "void" right where they stood. The fall foliage was colorful and inviting, bathed in brilliant sunshine; I imagined 1945 in only black and white and red, the latter representing the blood of the murdered and the Nazi flag. The air was fresh and clean; not so when my father arrived. Back then it smelled of rotting corpses and smoke and excrement.

I was surprised at how close to the camp the city of Dachau was. We entered the camp. My father had written about how the 116th Evac had "roared into Dachau." My entrance was more timid—and much quieter than a group of what looked like high school students who chattered aimlessly in a language I didn't understand.

My heart pounded. My hands shook. Part of it was simply knowing the horror that had gone on here; part of it, of course, was knowing that my father had once seen that very horror. I was walking in my father's footsteps. I was imagining the letters he'd written from this very place.

"I can't believe I'm here," I told Warren and Connie as we walked through the gate together.

We had arranged to meet with the director of research and an archivist. I had brought with me various news articles, pictures, and a few letters. Both staff members were polite and seemed very interested but not as excited as I was. They had arranged a tour for us but I really didn't want our time to end. That would change.

We toured the grounds where my father had spent five weeks in the spring of 1945. I was struck by the cold, gray, colorless barracks, concrete everywhere. One of the few touches of color were the flowers on the "tomb of unknown victims," whose ashes were ensconced within. We walked through the infamous "Work sets you free" gate, by the barracks, in an area where prisoners were forced to stand outside naked, regardless of the weather.

I felt a heaviness in my chest and a pit in my stomach, not what you need when the next stop was lunch. Eating at Dachau was a necessary evil, not a culinary experience. There was too much horrific history here to allow yourself to enjoy the pleasure of food, not when thousands starved to death at this very site. But something happened during the meal that made my day.

There was a polite tap on my shoulder.

"Excuse me."

I turned to see the director of research. She had walked the daunting length of the camp to find me.

"I'm so glad I found you," she said. "I would like you to come back and talk with me if you would, after the rest of your tour."

I was thrilled she had sought us out.

"I'd be glad to."

Later, we left our tour early so we could spend more time talking. She'd had time to read my articles and put things in perspective. Her interest made my heart soar; it gave me a deeper connection with my father.

"We have interviewed hundreds of liberators," she said, "but never a physician who'd been part of the liberators and stayed as long as your father and his colleagues had."

I felt honored to be the "voice of my father."

She asked more questions about him and his experience, about the letters. Then she offered us a private tour of some special areas, one of which included an exhibit about my father's friend, Hans Gerritsen. It included a pair of boots he had worn while, as a Dutch resister, he had been in the camp, detained as part of the Dutch intelligence service. Long after the war was over, he had been on the committee to establish the memorial at Dachau.

Gerritsen was a charismatic young man, known to the princesses of Dutch royalty as "Uncle Hans." He'd played on two Dutch national hockey teams. It was fascinating to see an exhibit about the one "good thing" my father had found at Dachau—Gerritsen. And it was satisfying to offer information about the man I'd found in my father's possession to the people who kept alive the camp's history.

Soon it was time to leave. It had been a long day, an emotional day, a good day that left me with an array of mixed emotions—the honor of being where my father had been, and the horror of understanding more clearly the atrocities that had taken place there. On our way out I saw the high school group that had been so chatty. Nobody was saying a word.

BACK HOME I first entertained the idea of perhaps writing a book. Doing it on my own seemed daunting, especially for an extrovert like me who would rather speak to a group of two hundred people than hunker down on a rainy night and write. From the minute I caught the vision to be my father's voice, though, I've sensed that I was not alone, that God kept whispering that He was in on this, too. Shortly before Christmas 2018, I met Bob Welch, a Eugene author and former *Register-Guard* newspaper columnist who mentors/edits other would-be authors. He had written a handful of World War II books, was intrigued by my father's stories, and was open to partnering with me on the project.

It was a fascinating and fearful, experience. Fascinating because he peppered me with so many questions over lunch salads that I learned all sorts of things about myself, my father, and World War II that I never would have otherwise. Fearful because just when he'd peel away another layer from the Clarice-and-her-father onion, just when I'd felt as if I didn't want to be any more vulnerable, he'd gently probe until another layer fell away.

I am extroverted in the sense that I like to be around people and enjoy speaking in front of crowds. Regarding my personal life, I'm extremely guarded, a legacy of my father's edict that I suppress all feeling. But Bob had a way of getting me to understand that burying emotions buries deeper truths that need telling—particularly for audiences who've experienced challenges similar to my own and could benefit from realizing they weren't alone. With the full support of my therapist, who met with the two of us, he helped me face some realities about my father that I hadn't been willing to accept. Among my most profound was the realization that telling a true story—even if the "leading character" has a dark side—didn't mean I was throwing him under the bus. Being honest about a flawed father could help the healing process for other families who had, or have, a war-scarred parent; in the end, that's what gave me the courage to finally wear my emotions on my sleeve.

That, frankly, was my biggest fear in this whole book project: that a reader might sense that my motive in writing this was revenge for the less-than-perfect father he was. If that were the case, why would I write a book whose main thrust is about how honorable and courageous the man was in World War II?

Discovering and absorbing the letters allowed me to see more fully the hero side of my dad and to understand more fully the experiences that led to his PTSD. Remembering my childhood allowed me to see the not-so-heroic side of the man. Reconciling the two sides of the man has never been easy. How could it be?

I was encouraged when Alexander, a trauma specialist in Eugene, heard of my deep struggle regarding whether to tell the full story of my father in the book. The therapy I've undergone, she said, isn't about me. It's about him. "All your reactions to what happened are natural. But what happened to you wasn't."

I'm through carrying his burdens and have come to realize that being honest with myself doesn't mean betraying him or anyone else. If this book offers lessons, among them is that we live in a world that's terribly imperfect; to a degree, we are all flawed. I've found my peace with my father. But he was, and still is, my father, a man who taught me the values of faith, purpose, and education.

What my father became after the war, within the confines of our family, does not negate what he once did for his country—for those who were part of his army medical staff, for soldiers—both American and German—and for the victims of Nazi persecution. How many of those former Dachau inmates owe their lives to my father and the dozens of other doctors who spent day after day trying to save the lives of people barely alive? How many who survived got to be reunited with a family or resume a career or go back to school or see a child or grandchild score a goal in a soccer game? Hans Garritsen said it himself: my father had saved his life.

What he didn't, or couldn't, give to his family does not negate what he *did* give to others—patients who survived because of his compassion, Boy Scouts who thrived because of him, Episcopalian parishioners whose faith deepened because of him.

Do I wish he could have treated our family like the others? Of course. But another hard, cold truth I learned on this journey was that the victims of war are not only those who die or are wounded. Victims are also those who *don't*—and nevertheless bring home emotional wounds that infect the people they love the most.

All the more reason why a government that pours so much time, money, and energy into preparing people for war should do considerably more to help them once they're home.

Chapter 17

Opening my own Pandora's Box taught me a multitude of lessons. I've learned that my father was right, the message of inhumanity throughout history can never be overemphasized. Even as my journey was unfolding, a staggering statistic—based on no fewer than 53,000 people in more than one hundred countries—was released, revealing that, nearly seventy-five years after the liberation of Dachau, two-thirds of the world's population either doesn't know the Holocaust happened—or deny it did. According to the survey done by the Anti-Defamation League, two-thirds of people in the world are ignorant of, or deny, the most staggering mass murder of all time, witnessed by millions and written about by thousands of others. (Goodreads alone lists 671 "well-written" books about the Holocaust.)

Much has been done to draw attention to such atrocities, but much more needs to be done. In 2017, neo-Nazi groups in America rose from ninety-nine to 121, marking a twenty-two percent increase. As identified by the Southern Poverty Law Center, the number of hate groups in America was up four percent to 954. In Germany alone, more than 4,000 attacks on foreigners and asylum hostels occurred between 2015 and 2019.

World War II is over, yes, but hate persists like an unchecked weed. It passes down from generation to generation, from place to place, from group to group, manifesting itself in different ways but fueled by the same kind of warped nationalistic fervor from which Dachau emerged.

Sadly, the farther we get from WWII, the experts tell us, the less real the atrocities of it become. The media report hate crimes daily. In a sense, exactly what my father feared might happen is, in fact, happening: people are forgetting how cruel people can be to one another. And that dilutes the safeguards to slow the spread of hate.

I've learned that we're being shortsighted to assume that the lesson of Dachau is limited to: "Never allow mass murders to happen." No, the lesson of Dachau is to not let hatred, bigotry, and cruelty get a foothold, period. Regardless of the scale. Regardless of the place. Regardless of the time. Humans have perpetrated atrocities on other humans since World War II ended: millions dead in the Congo, Cambodia, Somalia, Syria, Myanmar, and other countries ravaged by ethnic cleansings.

My father, of course, was speaking specifically of Dachau and similar atrocities masterminded by the Nazis in World War II; the majority of Germans weren't involved in the death and concentration camps. Many hid Jews during the war. But the broader lesson is to resist any person, any organization, any country that would dare to treat people with such indignity.

I've learned that people change and that war, in particular, changes people. If, as a country, we're going to send men and women off to war, we must accept this uncomfortable truth: the price we'll pay isn't simply in dead, wounded, MIAs, and POWs, but, when the battle is over, in the emotionally wounded who've returned home. More than twenty veterans a day take their lives, more than 6,000 a year. We are negligent if we don't understand the ongoing effects of war, commit to helping these soldiers, and give them a place to talk out their hidden wounds with those who understand. For whatever it promises in return, war always takes more than it gives.

Yes, sometimes war is necessary to stop the spread of evil; who knows what the world would be like had Hitler not been stopped? But since World War II, millions have died in wars whose purposes were far less cut-and-dry. How many would have been avoided if we had put an end to the "isms"—racism, anti-Semitism, class-ism, sexism, and on and on?

They begin with words. Speaking of Auschwitz, a survivor of the death camp, Bronia Brandman, told NBC in 2019, "I hope all people will know it started with words, words of hatred."

War not only opens the floodgates of inhumanity to the innocent—of the 75 million people killed in World War II, more than half were civilians—but inextricably changes those who must fight those wars.

I've learned compartmentalization and detachment didn't work for my father. Unlike with the trunk, he couldn't stuff Dachau in a box and hide it in the attic, never again to open it up. And he couldn't detach from his six months of war and five-plus weeks at Dachau.

I've learned that when we refuse to share our pain to others, it can embroil us, and those around us, in our own private wars. Telling your own story not only is therapeutic for you, it unlocks the stories of others—and that can be therapeutic for them. To be held back by fear is to assure that an important story isn't going to get told and that readers are going to miss the opportunity to be helped in coming to grips with their own similar experiences.

I've learned that my Christian faith beckons me to respond to the madness of the world—even if I don't understand why God might allow it to happen.

I've learned that the destiny of your journey might not be exactly where you originally thought it would be, but it might be exactly where you *need* to be. I began this project thinking my story was only about being the voice of my father regarding Dachau. But along the way I realized there were a couple of voices missing in my father's story. One belonged to my mother, who lost hers along the way because of a husband whose demands silenced her. And one belongs to me, a daughter who found hers long after her father had died. I've not used my voice to disparage the memory of my father, only to tell a further truth—in the same spirit in which he suggested light must be shined on those who would exploit others.

Finally, I've learned that daring to be open and honest about painful things can bring healing. Bullies hate having any sort of light shone on them because they don't want to be found out. As Russian and Allied troops closed in on concentration and death camps, why did the Nazis attempt to dismantle the camps and hide their crimes, blowing up gas chambers and marching their prisoners to far-away forests to shoot them? Why do child abusers threaten their victims? Why do evil-doers hate the bright lights of the media?

Because when silence prevails, bullies win. It's why my father pleaded with my mother to spread the message that the horrors of Dachau were real. It's why I wrote this book. In writing about war having already wrecked his manhood, my father said, "This is something for the world to think about!"

So, of course, was Dachau. Maybe that's why my father refused to throw out those letters during the fifty years he lived beyond the war. Because, if even subconsciously, he wanted to tell the world but could not. Dared not. Because to hold up a mirror to Dachau meant holding up a mirror to himself, and that was an image too painful for him to see.

During one of my talks, I said I was puzzled why my parents had kept the box of letters and never said anything about them. Afterward, a local physician—a medic in Vietnam—approached me.

"Your parents remembered the letters were there," he said. "They just couldn't talk about them. They hoped one day that one of their children would do something about the letters."

Now, one of their children has. It's true that when I found those letters and perused those pictures, it unleashed a Pandora's Box of sorts, at least for me personally. But I'm so glad I opened it.

There's a detail in the Pandora story of which some might be unaware. Zeus gifts the beautiful woman, Pandora, a box, yes, which she's told to never open—and when she does, out swarms all the troubles of the world, never to be recaptured. But one thing remains, stuck under the lid: hope.

When my father leaned over a patient in the Battle of the Bulge or at

Dachau, I like to think that's the ultimate gift he offered that man—the chance that he'd been given a second chance to life. And when we dare to confront the darkness of hate with light, I like to think that's what we offer the world.

Hope—that we can learn from our mistakes, that we can stop repeating the proverbial "sins of our fathers," and that our dreams of peace can come true.

Yes, *hope*. That, too, came in the box in the attic that introduced me to the father who I'd never known—and wished I had.

Acknowledgments

It takes a village to write a book. I offer my deepest gratitude to the following people without whom I couldn't have told my story as I did:

Bob Welch, for his talent, wisdom, and mentoring in helping me tell my story, and Sally Welch, for her support and, on occasion, for helping talk Bob down off the ledge. Debra Whiting Alexander, Ph.D, a mental health practitioner, offered amazing insight into my father. Dr. Tom Boubel, an anesthesiologist, was wonderful with his medical consultation. Ann Petersen and Jeff Wright edited with great precision. Tom Penix helped design a great cover. Beth Lazaro photocopied multiple pages of all 300-plus letters.

Others have helped me, as my father requested of my mother, "tell thousands" about the realities of Dachau: The Holocaust Center for Humanity in Seattle, Washington, for archiving the Wilsey Collection for public review. Their dedicated staff in particular: Dee Simon, Julia Thompson, Laurie Warshal Cohen, Richard Greene, and Sydney Dratel. Thank you for your commitment to teaching the world about the tragedy of the Holocaust and to Never Forget. Your commitment to incorporating my father's Dachau story in your museum and educational programming is greatly appreciated.

The Oregon Jewish Museum and Center for Holocaust Education and your amazing dedication to reminding the world, "Never Again."

The Holocaust Survivors of the Oregon Jewish Museum and Center for Holocaust Education speakers bureau. It is an honor to know each of you. Sharing your stories and promoting the message of Never Again are gifts you have given to those who lost their lives, and to those who survived.

To the people in both organizations, you have made a significant impact on the world and in my life.

Thanks, also, to the Second Generation group, for sharing the heartbreaking stories of your families during the Holocaust. I have learned much from each of you regarding the impact of the Holocaust on second generations.

To the Peck Stacpoole Foundation and Jay Margulies for reaching out to me and providing the finances to the Holocaust Center for Humanity in order to digitize my father's letters so the world would know the truth.

The students in the Museology Master of Arts Program and the Library and Information Sciences Program at the University of Washington for creating an effective and efficient retrieval system for accessing my father's handwritten documentation.

Barry Rubenstein, an attorney, was kind enough to help me gain legal ownership of the letters.

Thanks to my wonderful colleagues at the University of Oregon Career Center for your continual support, encouragement, and interest in my undertaking since I first saw my father's picture at the United States Holocaust Memorial Museum. Thank you for sharing in my excitement as the discoveries continued. Also, Pat Ferris, Hilary Vos, Kristin Grieger, Rick Guerra, James Chang, Jan Hart, Claire Richtman, Anne Hardin-Ballard, who are career development colleagues.

The schools, museums, synagogues, churches, libraries, and others who have invited me to share my dad's remarkable story regarding Dachau and the Battle of the Bulge.

More Villagers: I'm incredibly grateful for the talent, encouragement, listening, research, and prayers of the following people who've walked this journey with me in a variety of ways: Victoria McMillan, Linda and Dale Newton, Paula Smith, Lisa Hull, Cheryl Boyum, Shari Keyser, Joanne Jensen, Kathleen Verigin, Tina Enberg, Nena Strickland, Mary and Fred Van Ess, Kyle Santos, Helen Hepp, Louise Jacobus, Anne Haynes, Pam Raasch, Mary Hull, Jeff Burgess, Barb Krause, Pat Stroh, Sue Slaughter-Nichols, Megan Undeberg, Marshall Goldberg, Deborah Green, the Herron sisters, Warren Higer, Connie Mitchell, Katherine White, Andrea Heavrin, Molly DeBusschere, Gerrie Riihimaki, Emily Cohen, Sue and Bob Castagna, Barb Butterfield, Carol Wanamaker, Cheryl Dittamore, the Bernhardt Family, Doris and Hank Asmussen, St. Matthew's Episcopal Grace Group, Tuesday prayer partners, Bible Study Fellowship Group; to Julie Gemmell, M.D., Doug Austin, M.D., Audrey Garrett, M.D., Stewart Mones, M.D., and Anita Dekker, M.D., and Erik Verdouw, P.T.

Especially to the Holy Trinity for guiding this calling. And, finally, to Steve Friess, whose article in the *New Republic* opened up interest in my father's letters, which led to opportunities for me to share his story far and wide.

Thank you, all, with my deepest gratitude.

CLARICE WILSEY
EUGENE, OREGON
APRIL 2020

Bibliography

General Books

Abzug, Robert H. *Inside the Vicious Heart: Americans and the Liberation of Nazi Concentration Camps.* New York: Oxford University Press, 1985.

Barris, Ed. *Rush to Danger: Medics in the Line of Fire.* Toronto, Canada: HarperCollins Publishers Ltd., 2019.

Berben, Paul. *Dachau 1933-45: The Official History.* San Francisco: Norfolk Press, 1975.

Berg, Richard. *Scars: The Effects of Post Traumatic Stress on Families, Relationships and Work.* Chicago, Illinois: Corby Books, 2013.

Childers, Thomas. *Soldiers from the War Returning: The Greatest Generation's Troubled Homecoming from World War II.* New York: Houghton Mifflin Harcourt, 2009.

Cowdrey, Albert E. *Fighting for Life: American Military Medicine in*

World War II. New York: The Free Press, 1994.

Dann, Sam, editor. *Dachau 29 April 1945: The Rainbow Liberation Memoirs.* Lubbock, Texas: Texas Tech University Press, 1998.

Gawne, Johnathan. *Finding Your Father's War: A Practical Guide to Researching and Understanding Service in the World War II U.S. Army.* Haverston, Pennsylvania: Casemate Publishing, 2013.

Gruner, Wolf; translated by William Templar. *The Persecution of the Jews in Berlin 1933-1945: A Chronology of Measures By The Authorities in the German Capital.* Berlin: Stiftung Topographie des Terrors, 2014.

Levinson, Leila. *Gated Grief: The Daughter of a GI Concentration Camp Liberator Discovers a Legacy of Trauma.* Brule, Wisconsin: Cable Publishing, 2011.

Linderman, Gerald F. *The World Within War: America's Combat Experience in World War II.* New York: The Free Press, 1997.

Malarkey, Sgt. Don, with Bob Welch. *Easy Company Soldier: The Legendary Battles of a Sergeant From World War II's Band of Brothers.* New York, St. Martin's Press, 2008.

Matthews, Tom. *Our Father's War: Growing Up in the Shadow of the Greatest Generation.* New York: Broadway Books, 2005.

Parrish, John A., M.D. *Autopsy of War: A Personal History.* New York: St. Martin's Press, 2012.

Patton, General George S. *War As I Knew It.* New York: Houghton Mifflin Company, 1947. Renewed 1975.

Perry, Michael W., editor. *Dachau Liberated: The Official Report by the U.S. Seventh Army.* Seattle: Inkling Books, 2000.

Poldermans, Sophie. *Seducing and Killing Nazis.* SWW Press, 2019.

Sacco, Jack. *Where the Birds Never Sing: The True Story of the 92nd Battalion and The Liberation of Dachau.* New York: Harper Perennial Publishers, 2004.

Sites, Kevin. *The Things They Cannot Say.* New York: Harper Perennial, 2013.

Smith, Marcus J. *Dachau: The Harrowing of Hell.* Albany, New York: State University of New York Press, 1995

Tick, Edward. *War and the Soul: Healing Our Nation's Veterans from Post-traumatic Stress Disorder.* Wheaton, Illinois: Quest Books

(Theosophical Publishing House), 2005.

Vento, Carol Schultz. *The Hidden Legacy of World War II: A Daughter's Journal of Discovery.* Camp Hill, Pennsylvania: Sunbury Press, 2011.

Whitlock, Flint. *The Rock of Anzio: From Siciliy to Dachau: A History of the U.S. 45th Infantry Division.* Boulder, Colorado: Westview Press, 1998.

Wicks, Ben. *When the Boys Came Marching Home: True Stories of the Men Who Went to War and the Women and Children Who Took Them Back.* Toronto, Canada: Stoddart Publishing Co., Limited, 1991.

Books by Survivors

Bannister, Nonna, with Diana George and Carolyn Tomlin. *The Secret Holocaust Diaries.* Highlands Ranch, Colorado: Tyndale Press, 2009.

Brass Zauder, Karen. *Trauma Filters: A Second Generation Personal Account by the Daughter of Holocaust Survivor, David Zauder.* Pine, Colorado: Chazak Publishing, 2013.

Frank, Anne, translated by B.M. Mooyart-Doubleay. *The Diary of a Young Girl.* New York: Bantam Books, 1967.

Kern, Alice. *Tapestry of Hope.* Portland, Oregon: Limited Edition Club, 1988.

Wiesel, Elie. *Night.* New York: Hill and Wang, 1958.

Resources for Families with Veterans

For families that include a veteran and might be struggling with emotional issues linked to his or her having served—or currently serving—in the military, here are some resources to consider:

- Your physician
- Referral from friends for counselors/therapists
- Local and college veterans centers; Veterans Administration
- State Licensing Boards for; Psychologist or Social Workers or Counselors and Therapists or Marriage and Family Therapists
- DAV.org/ moral injury
- Compassionate Warriors
- Volunteers of America (veterans and moral injury support)
- Alcoholics Anonymous
- Al-Anon

- Church related family service departments
- Pastoral counselors
- Domestic Violence support groups
- Mental Health Insurance panels
- Sexual assault/abuse support groups

If you are a veteran or concerned about one, free, twenty-four-hour confidential support is available. Call the Veteran's Crisis Line at 1-800-273-8255 and Press #1, send a text message to 838255, or chat online. Go to: https://www.mentalhealth.va.gov/suicide_prevention/veterans-crisis-line.asp

www.ingramcontent.com/pod-product-compliance
Lightning Source LLC
Chambersburg PA
CBHW031108080526
44587CB00011B/877